A Translation of Plato's *Sophist* with an Introductory Commentary

New Perspectives in Philosophical Scholarship
Texts and Issues

James Duerlinger
General Editor

Vol. 4

PETER LANG
New York • Washington, D.C./Baltimore • Bern
Frankfurt am Main • Berlin • Brussels • Vienna • Oxford

A Translation of Plato's *Sophist* with an Introductory Commentary

TRANSLATED BY

James Duerlinger

PETER LANG
New York • Washington, D.C./Baltimore • Bern
Frankfurt am Main • Berlin • Brussels • Vienna • Oxford

The Library of Congress has cataloged the hardcover edition as follows:

Duerlinger, James.
Plato's Sophist: a translation with a detailed account of its theses and arguments / translated by James Duerlinger.
p. cm. — (New perspectives in philosophical scholarship; v. 4)
Includes bibliographical references.
1. Plato. Sophist. 2. Sophists (Greek philosophy). 3. Methodology. 4. Ontology.
I. Plato. Sophist. II. Title. III. Series: New perspectives in philosophical scholarship; 17.
B384.D84 184—dc22 2004006660
ISBN 978-0-8204-7417-5 (hardcover)
ISBN 978-1-4331-7665-4 (paperback)
ISSN 1045-4500

Bibliographic information published by **Die Deutsche Bibliothek**.
Die Deutsche Bibliothek lists this publication in the "Deutsche Nationalbibliografie"; detailed bibliographic data is available on the Internet at http://dnb.ddb.de/.

80 Broad Street, 5th floor, New York, NY 10004
www.peterlang.com

Table of Contents

Preface

In this second edition of Plato's *Sophist*, the commentary of the first edition has been extensively revised. As in the earlier commentary, I do not discuss the secondary literature in any detail, since the translation and commentary have been composed to introduce the theses and arguments of the dialogue to students in courses in Greek philosophy, Plato's philosophy, and the history of metaphysics, rather than to engage scholars in a debate concerning what these theses and arguments are. Scholarly arguments for my claims in the commentary I hope to present in a series of articles or in a scholarly tome, which is the more proper venue for their presentation.

Although numerous English translations of the *Sophist* have appeared in print, they do not, I believe, convey accurately the meaning of the central theses and arguments it contains. In particular, they invariably represent Plato as discussing the meaning of "what is not,""what is," and "is not," which I argue in the commentary are not accurate translations of Plato's own use of *to mē on, to on* and *ouk estin*, respectively, in the *Sophist*. It is for this reason that I have produced my own English translation of the dialogue for use by students, most of whom are completely dependent upon a translation for their understanding of what Plato says in the dialogue.

In the commentary, what is said in the dialogue is explained on the basis of what in the ancient world was considered to be Plato's own philosophy. This does not mean, however, that my explanation does not have important implications for the project of interpreting what is said on the basis of the technical terminology employed in contemporary philosophy. What these implications are is not explained here, lest the character of the commentary be compromised. The commentary is an attempt to explain what is said in the *Sophist*, as Plato would, in terms of his theory of forms and views about dialectic as they are explained in his middle period dialogues and by Aristotle and the later Platonists.

The attempt to explain what is said in the *Sophist* solely in terms of his theory of forms is rejected by some scholars on the ground that it is doomed to fail, since for various reasons they believe that we are no longer in a position to understand the original meaning of what Plato says in his dialogues. My reply to this reasoned pessimism is simply that one of the most important benefits of the study of the dialogues is the opportunity it provides us to attempt to see ourselves and our world as Plato does. This is one way in which we can loosen the stranglehold current philosophical concerns have upon our minds. An approach to the history of philosophy that formulates its problems solely in contemporary terms carries with it the danger of losing their original meaning.

Many scholars have tried to interpret the ideas and problems discussed in

Plato's dialogues with the help of technical philosophical terminology first developed at the beginning of the twentieth century. This approach to the dialogue has its own benefits, but it should not be pursued to the exclusion of the attempt to understand the original ideas and problems from the perspective from which they were originally presented. This is what I am attempting to do here. I believe that there are many who teach the history of philosophy who share my desire to study it in this way. This may be one reason the first edition, in spite of its flaws, sold out.

Some scholars have advanced theories about Plato's philosophy that have made it appear as if what is said in the *Sophist* cannot be understood on the basis of his theory of forms. One such theory is that Plato had already abandoned or at least significantly modified his theory of forms by the time he wrote the *Sophist.* Most scholars agree that the *Sophist* was composed after he composed the *Parmenides*, in which objections to the theory of forms are presented and do not seem to be answered in the dialogue. Many believe that Plato abandoned or at least modified his theory of forms on the basis of the objections to the theory of forms presented in the *Parmenides*. I believe that the objections are answered in the dialogue, but it is preferable for me to mount a defense of that belief in an article or book addressed specifically to other scholars. Whether or not it can be said that Plato had abandoned or significantly modified his theory of forms, of course, depends upon exactly how his theory is characterized and upon what counts as a significant modification. As I interpret his theory of forms in the commentary that follows, it has not been modified in any fundamental way. In fact, I believe, a close reading of the interpretation I give to Plato's theory here provides the clues to how he thinks that these objections are answered in the second part of the *Parmenides*.

Another theory that casts doubt on efforts to interpret what is said in the *Sophist* from the standpoint of Plato's theory of forms is that the dialogues are philosophical dramas he composed to stimulate thought rather than to represent his own point of view. Yet another is that the reports of Plato's oral teachings by Aristotle and ancient Platonists cannot be trusted to provide us with reliable information about how to interpret the theses and arguments contained in his dialogues. These theories have encouraged some contemporary scholars of Plato's philosophy to interpret what is said in the *Sophist* on the basis of later philosophical ideas. The adoption of either of these theories, I believe, inhibits our chance to understand properly what Plato is saying in the *Sophist*.

Many of my claims about Plato's views will be deemed by scholars as controversial and to require an elaborate defense. Since I do not present full arguments here for my claims about Plato's views, I suggest that students and scholars of Plato's philosophy who have reservations about my claims treat them as hypotheses they can test against what is said in the dialogues and by what the ancient scholars report Plato's philosophy to be. Care should be taken when testing my claims, however, not to read into the dialogues and ancient reports the interpretations the claims are meant to challenge. Should the testing of my claims lead to greater understanding of the *Sophist*, my efforts shall not have been in vain.

The numbers and letters in the margins of the translation refer to sections of the pages of the Stephanus edition of the Greek text. This is the standard way reference is made to passages in Plato's dialogues. Although their placement is not exact, they should enable readers who wish to consult the Greek text to find the text translated. Because of the inexactness of the placement of the numbers and letters in the margins, in the introductory commentary I do not cite the line numbers in my references to sections unless I explicitly cite the Greek words of the text I am citing.

I wish to express my thanks to John Cirignano for his expert help in the preparation of the translation, to Jennifer Wilson, John Finamore, Henry Teloh, Thomas Williams and Anthony Preus for their comments on the early versions of the first edition, and to Gina Chapleau for checking the commentary of this edition for typographical errors and stylistic infelicities.

James Duerlinger
University of Iowa
December 14th, 2008

Introduction

Why Plato Composed the *Sophist*

Plato seems to have written the *Sophist* in order to help his own students, who were already conversant with his theory of forms, to call to mind his teaching on two special uses of dialectic. The first is the use of its method of collection and division to define a sophist and the second is to use its method of derivation to refute a sophistic objection to a part of the definition. In the process of refuting the objection he draws upon his theory of forms to refute a number of what he considers to false metaphysical views held by his predecessors and contemporaries. The dramatic context of the *Sophist* suggests a third motivation. The discussion that takes place in the dialogue is represented in it as having occurred shortly before Socrates' trial, depicted in the *Apology*, at which Socrates is to defend himself against the charge of being a sophist who pretends to have knowledge of things divine. This context suggests that Plato also meant the *Sophist* to present an account of what a sophist is that would make it clear to his students that Socrates was not in fact a sophist.

This dramatic context of the dialogue also explains in part why Plato does not make Socrates his spokesperson. To make Socrates his spokesperson would clash with the representation of Socrates in the *Apology* as a simple seeker after virtue (*aretē*) who prods his fellow Athenians to act virtuously and to examine their claims to have knowledge of what the virtues are. This is the dramatic persona of Socrates in what are usually called the early period dialogues of Plato. In these dialogues Socrates is for the most part made to examine the beliefs of others, especially the sophists, concerning the different virtues of character and mind. In the early dialogues, *Meno* and the *Protagoras*, for instance, he has Socrates confute the sophists' claim that they teach virtue. In other early dialogues he has Socrates complain about the sophists' practice of charging a fee for the teaching of virtue. In the *Euthydemus* Socrates is made to poke fun at some of the verbal tricks used by sophists. To cite a more well-known example, in the first book of the *Republic*, which most scholars believe to have initially been an early dialogue, Socrates is also represented as refuting the sophistic view that justice is to the interest of the stronger.

The early period dialogues are contrasted by scholars to the middle period dialogues, in which Socrates is made to set out the theory of forms in an effort to define the virtues and explain how, in reliance upon the development of the virtues we can (i) escape rebirth, (ii) gain knowledge of the forms and the good, which is their first cause, and (iii) create a city state in which virtue is fostered. Even in the dialogues of this period Plato is concerned to deal with the sophists. For instance, in the *Theaetetus*, which is most likely a middle period dialogue, he has Socrates offer a refutation of Protagoras' famous sophistic doctrine, that man is the measure of all things, along with a refutation of the Heraclitean doctrine of flux that Plato seems to have believed was used by Protagoras to support the doctrine. Finally, in the late period dialogues, Plato has his spokespersons, who are usually not Socrates, defend his theory of forms and refute the views of other philosophers and the sophists.

In the *Sophist*, which is a late dialogue, facets of the activities of the sophists are incorporated into the first five attempts to define a sophist. Although in the sixth attempt he portrays a sophist as someone who possesses the art of refuting the conceit of wisdom, he makes it clear that this characterization is based on a false likeness a sophist has to Socrates. This false likeness is incorporated into Plato's final characterization of a sophist, according to which he is a person who possesses the skill to make himself appear to be wise by creating false images of truth in discourse.

Although readers who wish to understand what Plato says in the *Sophist* need to possess some knowledge of his theory of forms, an attempt to provide them with this knowledge is not an easy task, as is reflected by the fact that contemporary scholars have been unable to agree about what the theory is. This disagreement arises in part because most scholars rely almost exclusively on what is said in the dialogues to reconstruct Plato's theory, even though he himself implies in several places in his writings that his dialogues do not contain a full and careful statement of his philosophical views. For instance, he has Socrates in the *Phaedrus* at 274B–278B claim that written discourses are an improper way to teach others about the true natures of things, since such discourses cannot make themselves clear to those who do not already know what they are, and that they should be composed, if at all, only as an enjoyable pastime whose outcome will enable his students to call his teachings to mind.

The true divine creations of a dialectician are said to be his oral discourses, in which his students are individually shown how to gain knowledge of the true natures of things in a way they can retain this knowledge and defend their claims to knowledge from objections. In the *Seventh Letter*, at 341A–344D, moreover, Plato explicitly claims that he has written no serious philosophical work with the intention of informing others of the true natures of things, since the instruments used to obtain knowledge of these natures are imperfect and only students of great capacity can obtain it. Finally, because Plato's writing took the form of dialogues, in which his views are expressed in informal and ambiguous ways, it is not always possible for those not privy to his oral teachings to understand them simply on the basis of a study of his dialogues.

For these reasons, the views Plato expresses in the *Sophist* cannot be explained exclusively in reliance upon what he wrote in the dialogues. If we are to understand these views, therefore, we will need to call upon the reports of his oral teachings by his students and upon the distinctions these students employ in their own philosophical work when it seems likely that they were using the distinctions used by Plato himself. Our first and most important source for recovering Plato's oral teachings, therefore, are the reports by Aristotle, who was a student in Plato's Academy for twenty years. In addition, since Aristotle surely drew upon Plato's philosophy during these years to develop his own philosophy, we may assume that many distinctions made by Aristotle in his written work are likely to have been borrowed from Plato himself. Here I will employ not only Aristotle's reports of Plato's oral teachings, but also some of the distinctions made by Aristotle when they help us to understand Plato's informal and often ambiguous expression of his philosophy in the *Sophist*. Such distinctions can help us to reconstruct what Plato actually means in passages that are otherwise difficult to interpret.

Since there are still a number of passages in the *Sophist* that Aristotle's reports and distinctions do not help us to interpret, we need also to turn to our next best ancient source for Plato's philosophy, the reports and interpretations provided by the later Greek Platonists. These Platonists most likely had access to various traditions of the transmission of Plato's oral teachings, which may have been created on the basis of Plato having individually tailored what he said to meet the needs of the different students he had. Not all of the later Platonists reports of what Plato taught, of course, need be correct, especially those that clearly contradict what would appear to be Plato's most basic tenets.[1] Where their reports do not contradict one another and would seem, for historical and philosophical reasons, to reflect more accurately what Plato wrote in the dialogues, I think that it is reasonable to use them to help us understand what Plato has his characters say in the *Sophist*. In this introductory commentary and its notes and in the notes to the translation, therefore, these secondary sources are being used to facilitate a reconstruction of the meaning of the theses and arguments Plato expresses in the *Sophist*.

My approach to the explanation of the theses and arguments in the *Sophist* is unfashionable and thought to be fraught with dangers. I believe that the more fashionable approach, which is to rely on contemporary ideas to interpret what Plato says, for instance, about the uses of *to mē on*, *to on*, and *estin*, has led us into a dead end and that the dangers of relying upon the reports of Aristotle and the later Platonists have been exaggerated. If progress is to be made in our efforts to understand this difficult dialogue, I believe, we must face these dangers. Let my approach be judged by its fruits.

Plato's *Sophist* is naturally divided into two parts. In the first, he uses dialectic to define a sophist, and in the second, which interrupts the first, he uses dialectic to expose the erroneous reasoning a sophist may use to try to undermine a key element of the definition. In this introduction I will discuss the first part as a whole, ignoring the fact that it is interrupted by the second, and then discuss the second part.

PART ONE

THE DEFINITION OF A SOPHIST

(216A–236C, 264D–268D)

The introductory conversation (216A–218E)

At the end of the discussion portrayed in the dialogue, *Theaetetus,* Socrates asks Theodorus[2] and Theaetetus[3] to meet with him again the next morning to continue their conversation. The *Sophist* recounts the discussion that takes place at this meeting. Theodorus has brought along an unnamed stranger from Elea, the home city of Parmenides. Theodorus introduces him as a mature philosopher trained in the Eleatic tradition. This stranger becomes Plato's spokesperson in the dialogue. I have followed the lead of Theodorus and call him the philosopher.

In the course of the opening conversation, the philosopher is persuaded to show those who are present how to distinguish a philosopher, statesman, and sophist from one another according to their natures. To distinguish them from one another according to their natures is to define what their natures are. In the *Sophist* itself Plato's spokesman shows Theaetetus how to define a sophist belongs, and in the *Statesman* how to define a statesman. Plato surely intended to write another dialogue in which the philosopher was to show Theaetetus how to define a philosopher, but we have no evidence that he wrote this dialogue. Since a sophist will be shown in the *Sophist* to be a false likeness of a wise man, rather being a mere semblance of one, it would seem that Plato is at least indirectly telling us in the *Sophist* itself that a philosopher is one who is in fact a true likeness of a wise man.[4]

It is significant that Plato has the philosopher come from Elea, where dialectic was born and raised in its early years. The father of dialectic, he believes, is Parmenides of Elea. In the dialogue, *Parmenides*, Plato shows respect to Parmenides by having him, portrayed as an old man, demonstrate a sophisticated form of dialectic for Socrates, who is portrayed as a young man who has just developed the theory of forms but has not yet acquired the ability to defend the theory against the objections to which it seems to be subject. Parmenides himself is made to present these objections to the theory, and then to teach the young Socrates how to use a special form of dialectic that will enable him to answer the set of objections that have been raised.

In the *Sophist*, Plato seems to be once again acknowledging his debt to father Parmenides. He has one of the philosophers in the Eleatic school, trained in a form of dialectic that assumes the existence of forms, show Theaetetus (i) how to define a sophist, (ii) how to refute an objection a sophist would have to the definition, and, in the process, (iii) how to refute the thesis upon which the objection is based, the thesis that father Parmenides himself had once believed was cornerstone of his argument for his claim that all things are one. Plato sees himself as the rightful heir to the practice of the art of dialectic first created by father Parmenides in Elea. In the *Sophist* he pays homage to its birthplace by having a philosopher from Elea be his spokesman.[5]

The philosopher agrees to guide Theaetetus by a skillful use of questions to a definition of the attribute the sophist possesses by its own nature. He first tells Theaetetus at 218C that their immediate purpose is to define what it is by reference to which they call someone a sophist. Plato believes that what it is by reference to which something is called a sophist is that which is a sophist by its own nature. What a sophist is by its own nature I will call its defining attributes. In general, what possesses a defining attribute is what Plato calls a form (*eidos*) or idea (*idea*).[6] We may define a Platonic form as (i) what is what it is by its own nature, i.e. what has defining attributes, and (ii) what causes everything that partakes of it to possess its attributes, though not as its defining attributes. Everything other than the form that possesses defining attributes possesses its attributes by virtue of partaking of the form.

In general, Plato seems to believe that forms are things that by their own natures are subjects in which universals are present or of which universals are predicated.[7] The term, "universal" (*katholou*) was introduced by Aristotle and defined as that which is by nature said of many things, where what is said of many things are the universals present in them or predicated of them. That Plato's forms are universals said of subjects, however, is the view held by most scholars. By contrast, the interpretation adopted here is that Plato posits the existence of forms in order to provide a subject of which universals are said in the above sense. So I deny, for instance, that Plato thinks that a man is just because he partakes of the universal, justice. Instead, Plato believes that a man is just because he partakes of that which is just by its own nature.

Plato seems to have adopted this view of the forms because he believes that (i) sensible things do not possess fixed natures of their own on the basis of which they possess defining attributes; (ii) if discourse and thought are to be possible, there must be things that possess natures of their own on the basis of which possess defining attributes; and (iii) discourse and thought are not applicable to sensible things unless they partake of things that by their own natures possess defining attributes. Hence, what is defined when a sophist is defined is what the form, the sophist, is by its own nature, not a universal present in or predicated of that form. The definition is of the defining attributes of the form, the sophist, not of anything else, since all forms possess different defining attributes, and nothing in the sensible world possesses a nature of its own on the basis of which it possesses defining attributes.

But if Plato's forms are not universals, why do most scholars believe that they are? One reason is that they assume that Aristotle attributes to Plato the view that forms are universals. They think this is so in spite of the fact that Aristotle repeatedly says that Plato believes that the forms are substances and that they are exemplars for the production of the sensible objects that partake of them. What Aristotle actually says, moreover, is not that Plato's forms are universals, but that the forms have "the same name" as that which is said of many sensible things.[8] He says this because Plato actually does often call forms by the names of the universals said of them by their own natures. He does not say this he believes because Plato thinks that all forms are universals. Plato, moreover, does not call all forms by the names of the universals said of them. I need to explain, of course, why Plato calls some forms by the names of universals said of them, since without this explanation, the natural assumption is that he thinks that these forms are universals.

Plato seems to have adopted the practice of calling a form that is the subject of a universal present in it by the name of the universal present in it because this type of form is recollected by us as the universal that is attributed to it. We recollect a form by means of conceiving the universal by means of which it is conceived because we are unable directly to apprehend the form when we recollect it. Since we recollect a form by means of conceiving the universal attributed to it, we refer to the form by means of the name of this universal. Hence, we refer to the form, that which is just by its own nature, as "justice." It is not clear, however, whether a form that is by its own nature the subject of a universal predicated of it, such as the species and genus to which it belongs, is or is not called by the name of the species or genus to which it belongs, since there is no indefinite article in Greek. Hence, that which is a man by its own nature might be said in English to be man or a man.

One incongruity of the view that a Platonic form is a universal is the fact that Plato sometimes predicates a universal of a form that he calls by the name of that same universal. Scholars call this "self-predication," and attempt to explain, with little success, in my opinion, why Plato would say of a universal that it is predicated of itself. An example of such a self-predication is "Justice is just." The explanation of why Plato says that justice is just, according to the present interpretation, is that what we conceive as justice is that which is just. It is, in fact, that which alone is just by its own nature, and is recollected by means of the universal said of it, since it is not being directly apprehended.

Plato employs a variety of names for forms. Sometimes he makes a name by adding a definite article to the name of the universal predicated of a form by its own nature, as he does with "the man" (*ho anthrōpos*) and "the being" (*to on*).[9] Sometimes he names a form by adding a definite article to an adjective to signify the form in which a universal is present by its own nature, as he does with "the just" (*to dikaion*) and "the other" (*thateron*). However, as we have seen, he also employs an abstract noun that signifies the universal present in a form by its own nature to create the name of the form, as he does with "otherness" (*heterotēs*) and "being" (*ousia*).[10]

In the *Phaedo*, Socrates is in effect made to say that his inquiry into the cause of universals being said of sensible objects requires that he take refuge in discourse (*logos*) about them rather than in perception (*aisthēsis*) of them.[11] Plato has Socrates say this because he believes that the ultimate subjects of discourse are the forms, and that when in discourse a universal is said of sensible things, it is said of them in dependence upon the universal being said of a form, since the cause of a universal being said of sensible objects is that they partake of the form of which the universal is said. As Socrates says in the *Phaedo*, the cause of a sensible object being beautiful is that it partakes of the form, the beautiful, which is, he implies, beautiful by its own nature.[12]

Plato believes that a man is called a sophist by reference to the form, a sophist, in which a man participates, and that by defining the form that is a sophist by its own nature, we are better able to determine whether or not a particular man, for instance, Socrates, partakes of this form. The need to arrive at definitions is important in dealing with sophists, Plato assumed, since their favorite trick is to equivocate on the use of terms in their arguments in order to create the impressions that a false statement follows logically from true statements, and that they are wise men. The method used in the *Sophist* to formulate the definition of a sophist Plato calls collection and division.

Dialectic and the method of collection and division

The method of collection and division to define forms is one of three methods employed in dialectic. First let us discuss what dialectic is, and then, the method of collection and division, along with the other methods employed in dialectic to accomplish different ends.

In his account of dialectic in the *Republic*, at 532A–534E, Socrates refers to dialectic as a line of investigation that "systematically attempts and in all cases to determine what each thing is," and the dialectician as "the man who is able to give an account of the substance [*tēs ousias*] of each thing." The substance of each thing is the form after which it is named. An account of this substance is a definition of the form. Since Socrates does not in the *Republic* explain the actual nature, purposes, and methods of dialectic, it may in fact contain more than the use of collection and division to define a form. In fact, the method of collection and division is the only method presented in the dialogues for arriving at a definition of a form.

In the *Sophist* itself, the philosopher presents a more general account of dialectic than the account Socrates presents in the *Republic*. It is an account that includes more than the use of the method of collection and division to define the forms. If we are to understand the nature, purpose, and methods of dialectic in this broader sense and the role it has to play within Plato's philosophy, we will need to rely to a certain extent on a reconstruction that includes reference not only to Plato's accounts in the dialogues, but also to the accounts given by Aristotle and the later Platonists. I will outline here a systematic reconstruction that I believe will help readers to understand what Plato says about dialectic not only in the *Sophist*, but also in the *Republic*, *Theaetetus* and *Statesman*.

In its fully expanded sense, the Platonic dialectic seems to be the art of using discourse to guide others to knowledge of the causal powers all things possess by virtue either of being the form, being, or what partakes of this form. As Plotinus explains Plato's dialectic in *Enneads*, I.3, it is a developed capacity, grounded in knowledge of the nature of the good and of the world of forms, to use discourse according to proscribed methods to define the different kinds of forms, to establish their relationships to the good and to one another, and to justify the first principles of the different special forms of knowledge recognized by Plato. The good, Plato believes, is the first cause of all things, both sensible and intelligible. An accomplished dialectician is he who has this developed capacity, which Plato himself calls dialectical knowledge.

Dialectical knowledge is developed for at least three different purposes. The first and most important of these purposes is to facilitate the attainment of the highest human good. The highest human good, Plato believes, is the divine life (*theios bios*), which in the *Phaedo* and *Phaedrus* he urges all to pursue. This is a life of contemplation of the good or the one, which he thinks is the first cause of the divine mind and its ideas. The divine life is the ultimate goal of the Platonic philosophy, the final escape from rebirth and the recovery of the soul's birthright. There are two forms of the divine life, that of the soul after she has escaped the body, and that of the still embodied soul that has achieved the vision of the good as a result of the ascent made possible by the practice of the upward phase of dialectic. The dialectician, by employing the methods of dialectic, leads the student upward to knowledge of the nature of the good that is confirmed by the vision of the good. Once the student achieves this vision and is established in it, he will not reincarnate again. After his vision of the good he is to turn his attention to the justification of the first principles of the special forms of knowledge, which are the principles he employed when climbing to the peak of the upward path.

The justification of the first principles upon which the special forms of knowledge are based is the second purpose for which dialectical knowledge is developed. These include not only the forms of knowledge mentioned in the *Republic* itself, which are mathematics, knowledge of number and calculation, as well as the geometries of planes, solids, solids in motion, and the harmonies produced by solids in motion, but also knowledge of logic and language, as well as ethics, politics, and theology, which are the forms of knowledge that pertain to the good for human beings, the good for the communities in which they live, and the good for their immortal souls.

Another purpose for which dialectic is developed is the "refutation" (*elenchos*) of false views about the nature of things. It is by virtue of Socrates' reputed mastery of this use of dialectic that in the *Theaetetus* he is able to present refutations of the views that knowledge is perception, that man is the measure of all things, and that all things without exception are in motion. Again, in the *Sophist*, it is by virtue of the philosopher's mastery of this dialectical ability that he is able to present refutations of the views that being cannot be other than motion and rest, that non-being cannot be, and that falsehoods cannot be. Plato believes that the refutation of these views and of pernicious views about morality taught by the sophists, rhetoricians and poets (refutations of which he presents in the *Protagoras*, *Gorgias*, and *Republic*) is required if we are to gain the insights we need in order to attain the divine life, which is the ultimate end for the sake of which dialectic is practiced.

Initially, however, refutation is used by a dialectician to enable us to abandon the conceit of wisdom. Therefore, as explained in the *Meno*, its use should instill in us the desire to learn to see things the way they really are, for if we already think we know, we cannot be taught. This is part of what is usually called the Socratic purpose of dialectic and it is the last of the three purposes of its development.

In the *Phaedrus*, at 264E–266B, a general characterization of the use of the method of collection and division to formulate definitions is presented. We may assume, on the basis of what Plato says in this dialogue about a collection, that it involves a survey of different genera said of forms for the purpose of determining what the genus of the definition of the form will be. In the *Sophist* itself, we shall see, the philosopher collects different genera of things said of a sophist and examines them for the purpose of determining which of them is the genus in the definition of a sophist.

Each form, Plato believes, has a nature that it alone possesses and is the basis upon which a universal is said of it. The universal said of the form by its own nature is said of all things that partake of the form, though it is not said of them by their own natures. Of the universals said of a form, one is the basis upon which it is named. This universal Plato calls by the same name he uses to refer to the form itself. This universal is usually translated as "species." One of the reasons that scholars have thought that Plato thinks that forms are universals is that Plato uses *eidos* to refer both to a form and to the universal after which the form is named. Since Plato does mean sometimes to refer to a species when he uses *eidos*, I will translate *eidos* as "species" when he uses it to refer to a species.

In the *Sophist* Plato also uses the expression, "the greatest kinds" (*megistē genē*) to refer to the forms of being, motion, rest, the same and the other. He calls these "the greatest kinds," it seems, because, like genera, which are universals to which all species belong, they are forms of which all other forms partake. Although I follow the customary translation of *megistē genē* as "the greatest kinds," Plato, I believe, here uses *genē* to refer to forms of which all other forms partake rather than to genera, which are universals predicated of the species to which the forms belong.

Since being is one of the greatest kinds, all forms other than being partake of it. Because all other forms partake of it, the others are not beings by their own natures. Likewise, as it is explicitly argued in the *Sophist,* since all forms other than the other, which is what by its own nature is other in relation to something else, are other than something else because they partake of this form, the others are not other than one another by their own natures. Since this can be said of all of the greatest kinds, it is clear that they are not the highest genera to which the different species of forms belong. They are what in *Metaphysics* XIV, Chapter 2, Aristotle refers to as "the elements" of all forms. Hence, when Plato has the philosopher search for the genus to which the species predicated of the form, the sophist, belongs, he will not be considering the greatest kinds as relevant to the search.

Some scholars have attempted to reconstruct the method of collection on the basis of an analysis of *Phaedrus* 249B–C, *Sophist* 253D, *Statesman* 258A–B, and *Philebus* 16B–17A, but these passages do not clearly explain it. Plato says much more in the dialogues about the method of division, but his comments about this method tend to be incomplete and vague. So we are fortunate to have Aristotle's account of Platonic division, and with the help of the terminology he employs I think that it can be described in some detail.

In a division, the highest genus to which a species belongs is divided by its differentiae into the kinds that are its parts, which are in turn again divided in this way, until a species that is not itself a genus is reached. The parts of a genus may be called its subdivisions, each of which is comprised of the genus itself and the differentia that distinguishes it from the other subdivisions. The subdivision under which the species immediately falls may be called the proximate genus of the species. The original genus is subdivided until the proximate genus is reached, and when its differentia is combined with it, a definition of the species to which a form belongs is reached. In this way the species is distinguished from all other species that falls under its proximate genus. In the *Phaedrus*, at 256B, Socrates claims to be a lover of such collections and divisions, and calls the practitioner of the method, who has the ability to discern the one and the many, a dialectician.

The method of collection and division is illustrated in the *Sophist* and the *Statesman*, and to some extent in the *Phaedrus*. It would seem to have at least two uses to which it can be put. The first is to present a definition of the form by arriving at the species to which a form belongs. Contrary to appearances, however, in this use it is, in the hands of the dialectician, a method of exposition rather than a method of discovery. A dialectician, who already has dialectical knowledge, teaches a student, who lacks knowledge of a form and seeks knowledge of the form, how to define the form by determining the species to which it belongs. The teacher asks the student questions he is to answer to the best of his ability in accord with his own degree of recollection of the form and its relations to other forms. In this way the student arrives at a discursive knowledge (*dianoia*) of the form.

At this point, the student's understanding of the definition of a form is based on an awareness of the likenesses and differences a form has to other forms rather than on a direct awareness of the form itself. But his awareness of these likenesses and differences is a prerequisite for gaining intuitive knowledge (*noēsis)* of the form. In the *Seventh Letter*, at 244B, Plato says that a student's discursive knowledge of the natures of things is brought about by training at the hands of an accomplished dialectician, and that this knowledge becomes intuitive knowledge when his mind suddenly becomes flooded with the light in which the forms themselves are directly revealed.

The use of the method of collection and division to define the forms is a very important part of dialectic, since no progress can be made in philosophy, Plato believes, unless inquiry begins with definitions. In the *Sophist*, Plato has the philosopher play the role of a dialectician who teaches Theaetetus, a student of dialectic, how to employ the method of collection and division to define a sophist.

Theaetetus is led through different attempts to define a sophist in order to enable him to discover, on the basis of the characterizations collected, causal powers a sophist possesses on the basis of which these characterizations are true of a sophist. The definitions collected on the way to the final definition are in fact incidental properties of a sophist. Having learned what a sophist is, Theaetetus is in a better position to avoid confusing him with a statesman or a philosopher, whose forms are to be distinguished from that of a sophist.

In the *Philebus*, at 16B–17A, Plato justifies his practice of defining the forms by claiming that forms themselves are both one and many. Plato thinks that the forms are both one and many because of the presence in them of "the limit" (*peras*), which causes them to be one, and "the unlimited" (*apeiron*), by virtue of which they are many.[13] He also thinks that forms are both one and many on the basis of the reasoning in the *Parmenides*, at 137C–166B, which leads him to the view that we cannot attribute anything to what is absolutely one and without parts. In the *Sophist*, this view underlies the philosopher's argument against the thesis that there is just one being.

In the *Phaedrus* at 270C–E, Plato has Socrates briefly explain how to reflect about the natures of things. Socrates is in effect explaining the most important principles underlying the discovery of the differentiae that divide genera into the species to which something belongs. If we want to know a thing's nature and to show it to others, Socrates is made to say, we must begin by determining whether the thing is or is not composite. (A thing is composite, he assumes, if it possesses parts into which it passes away.) If it is in fact composite, we are to continue to divide the thing until we reach parts that are not composite in this sense. These parts are then to be examined to determine what their causal powers are. The causal powers to which he refers are those on the basis of which they are defined.[14]

In the *Sophist*, the form of a sophist is considered to be an incomposite entity of the above sort, and the species to which it belongs is defined in terms of the causal powers the form possesses. The definition includes reference to the means by which these powers are exercised, the various kinds of objects their exercise concerns, the manner in which these powers are to be exercised, the instruments used to exercise them, the purpose to be achieved by their exercise, and so on. The trial division of the kind of skill the angler possesses is a good example of the principles that underlie the choice of the contrary differentiae that divide a genus. The principles used by Plato to divide the genera of the species to be defined into their differentiae are based on what he believes to be the causal powers of the form whose species is being defined.

In the *Sophist* and *Statesman*, Plato occasionally pauses to give advice about the use of the method of collection and division. In the *Statesman*, at 226D, as well as in the *Sophist*, at 227A–C, Plato points out that the worth or dignity of species and genera is irrelevant to the question of whether or not they may be used to classify a form. In the *Statesman* he also claims, at 262A–264B, that whenever possible a genus is to be divided into two natural subdivisions of equal size rather than into unequal subdivisions or into many small artificial subdivisions, making sure that each subdivision is a real kind of thing. At 267C–268B he says that a complete account of a species must distinguish it from the other species of the same genus. At 283B–287D he says that the length of a definition, just as the length of an argument, must be deemed appropriate by its success in enabling the species to be discerned rather than by some other criterion. Finally, at 287B, Plato adds that although some genera resist being divided into two natural subdivisions, those that do must be divided into as few subdivisions as is possible.

There are two more kinds of methods the dialectician employs in addition to the method of collection and division. There is, secondly, the method of hypothesis, which is the method used to solve problems that arise in the special forms of knowledge and, eventually, to arrive at knowledge of the good. The use of a hypothesis occurs in the *Meno*, where it facilitates an attempt to answer the question of whether or not virtue can be taught. The hypothesis employed is that virtue is knowledge, and its use is abandoned when an apparent counter-example is presented.

The method is explained at 99D–101E in the *Phaedo*, where Socrates introduces the hypothesis that there are forms that are what they are by their own natures to see if it can help him to determine whether or not the soul is immortal. He says that the point of making such a hypothesis is to investigate what does and does not agree with it and to consider as true what agrees and as false what does not. What he means by what agrees with the hypothesis, I believe, is what is proved by the hypothesis, and by what does not agree with the hypothesis is what disproves the hypothesis. Hence, since the hypothesis that there are forms, he goes on to argue, yields the conclusion that the soul is immortal, he regards that conclusion as true. Socrates adds that if a hypothesis such as the one he uses to prove that the soul is immortal is challenged, it must be established, in turn, on the basis of another hypothesis, and that hypothesis in turn established by another, and so on, until what in the *Republic* he calls "an unhypothetical first principle" is reached that establishes the initial hypothesis as true. In the *Republic,* at 510B–511D, the ultimate purpose of the application of this method to the hypothesis about the existence of forms is claimed to be the discovery of the first cause of all things.

The method of hypothesis, therefore, seems to have two parts. The first is to formulate a hypothesis that seems compelling and to find out whether or not it can be used to prove that something has a certain property. The second part of the method is to employ a more basic hypothesis to establish the truth of the first hypothesis, and if necessary, another to establish its truth. By following this method, according to Plato, we eventually arrive at a hypothesis concerning the highest principle, the first cause of all phenomena, whose truth is established not by another hypothesis, but by rational insight (*nous*).[15] When in the *Republic* Plato has Socrates say that in the first phase of the practice of dialectic one proceeds "upward" to the good, the means by which one proceeds upward is the use of the method of hypothesis.

The method of hypothesis and the method of collection and division are the means by which one who aspires to be a dialectician defines the forms, organizes the forms into hierarchical relationships, and finally locates and has a vision of their first principle. When he has mastered the layout of the world of divine mind contemplating its ideas and has arrived at the correct hypothesis concerning the first principle of this world, the student of dialectic, Plato seems to believe, needs to contemplate the principle in relation to everything that arises from it until this contemplation gives rise to an intuitive knowledge of the one or the good itself.

The third method employed in dialectic is the method of derivation. Because the dialectician is one who has acquired intuitive knowledge of the one or the good, he can demonstrate certain truths about the world of the divine mind and its ideas. He can demonstrate, for instance, that because of the natures that certain forms have, they can or cannot combine. He can prove, presumably, that virtue partakes of that which by its own nature can be taught, by establishing that virtue is a kind of knowledge, and that knowledge partakes of that which by its own nature can be taught. He can also show that a form whose being is denied by a sophist is in fact a being. This is exactly what Plato has the philosopher do in the *Sophist*. Plato has the philosopher argue that Parmenides' denial, that non-being is a being, is false, by proving that non-being is a being. He proves that non-being is a being by showing that non-being is that which is by its own nature other than something that is a being, and that non-being, so defined, partakes of being.

By whom is this capacity, this dialectical ability, to be developed? We know from many sources, especially the *Republic*, *Phaedrus*, *Symposium* and *Seventh Letter*, that it can be developed only by a certain type of student, and that he must be tested before receiving such training. The student must show that he perceives the beauty of both himself and the world, loves all forms of knowledge, has strength and nobility of character, is high spirited, has a good memory, and has various other intellectual abilities before he is allowed to begin this undertaking. In brief, only a student who has already made progress in the development of the virtues of character and mind is a suitable candidate. Two tests are used to see whether he meets the qualifications: does he live in accord with the principles taught by Plato and does he respond well to the examination of his beliefs? In the *Theaetetus* Socrates tests Theaetetus to see whether or not he is a suitable student of dialectic. Because he passes the test, in the *Sophist* Theaetetus is selected as the student to be taught by the philosopher how to use the method of collection and division and the method of derivation.

The definition of an angler (218E–221B)

Since the defining attributes of the sophist are difficult to discern, the philosopher suggests that they first practice the method of arriving at a definition on an easy case. The easy case chosen is its use to define an angler. In this way the philosopher provides an illustration of both the method of collection and division and the sort of definition that results from its employment. It is made obvious, with the aid of an explicit collection, that the angler is a man who possesses a skill or art (technē). The nature of an angler as an angler is the skill he possesses by virtue of which he is called an angler. Consequently, the quest for a definition of an angler becomes a search for an account of his skill, and the genus from which the search is to begin is skill itself. A brief collection is then used to determine the subdivisions of this genus, since they are not immediately obvious. By a survey of various skills the philosopher brings Theaetetus first to discern, as one subdivision of skill, skill in producing things, and as another, skill in acquiring them. Since both types seem to be divisions of what the philosopher in the Statesman, at 258E (cp. Republic, 532B) calls practical or applied skill, we should interpret "skill" here to mean "practical skill" rather than "art" or "skill" generally, since theoretical skills such as skill in mathematics are not included. Moreover, as many of the philosopher's examples make clear, we should not expect that there will always be a conventional name for each skill or that for every skill there is a conventionally designated art, since most conventional arts in fact involve many different skills. Although Plato may choose a genus and divide it by calling upon a conventional distinction, he apparently does so only when the distinction mirrors a likeness and difference he himself believes actually functions to distinguish a form from others in the same genus.

An angler is shown to be a person who has the skill to acquire (rather than to produce) by conquest (rather than by exchange) in the form of hunting (rather than competing with others) living things (rather than things that do not move themselves) that swim (rather than walk on land) in the water (rather than on the water) by striking them (rather than trapping them) with hooks alone (rather than with hooks and firelight) from below (rather than from above). An angler's skill is here progressively classified in more and more detail, until it is marked off from all other practical skills, and he is defined as being someone who possesses this skill.

The first five definitions of a sophist (221C–226A)

When the method of division is applied to the task of defining a sophist, the genus chosen to be divided is once again skill or art, and this genus is divided a number of times to arrive at definitions of the different kinds of skill a sophist possesses or seems to possess. The purpose of formulating definitions of the different kinds of skills a sophist possesses is to facilitate a recognition of which skill is most pertinent to the final definition.

The characterization of an angler as a hunter of a certain kind calls to mind a parallel skill of a sophist. While an angler hunts fish, a sophist hunts rich young men. His method of capturing them is to persuade them to pay him money for teaching them how to achieve virtue. Before the question can be raised about whether this sort of skill is the one that is essential to someone being a sophist, attention is called to yet another of his skills, which came to light near the end of the division, that of persuading others to pay him money for his teachings. Earlier, skill in acquiring things had been divided into skill in acquiring them by conquest and skill in acquiring them by exchange. This division calls to mind the idea that a sophist is skillful in conquering young men *because* he is so good at selling them the knowledge of virtue he claims to teach. If the sort of knowledge he sells is purchased in another city, he may be classified as a kind of merchant, if purchased in his own city, as a kind of retailer, and if he produces the knowledge himself, as a kind of manufacturer who sells his own product. Presumably, a sophist would be classified in all three ways if he sold knowledge of all three types.

The fifth definition introduces, in turn, the skill *because of which* a sophist is good at selling his product, his skill in overcoming young men in verbal combat by the use of disputation. From this point of view, his skill may be defined as skill in disputation with young men about all things in order to overcome them for a profit.

A sophist has been shown to possess skill in hunting young men, selling them knowledge of virtue, whether purchased in the same city, another city, or self-produced, and subduing them in disputations about all things, each for the sake of making money. Five definitions of a sophist have been formulated on the basis of his possession of these skills, and all, so to speak, call attention to ignoble aspects of his activities.

The sixth definition (226A–231B)

The sixth definition of a sophist, the philosopher says, shows a noble lineage, since in it he appears under the guise of being an educator who purges the conceit of wisdom from the souls of others by the use of the method of refutation. This definition proceeds from the subdivision, skill in separating things, examples of which are skill in sifting, straining, carding, spinning, and so on.

In the *Statesman*, at 282B–283B, the philosopher says that skill in combining things and skill in separating things have universal application, and he distinguishes the separative skills of sifting, straining, and so on, from weaving, which is a skill in combining things. But skills in combining and separating things, since of universal application, are note a unique subdivision of any other practical skill, and some skills, for instance, wool working and dialectic, include both. Since these skills are not included within Plato's schemes of classification of the genera of skills, they will be included, nonetheless, among the natures of the contrary forms that Plato uses to differentiate these genera.

Skill in separating things is divided into skill in separating like things from like and skill in separating things worse from things better. The philosopher calls the second of the two "skill in purging things," and divides it into gymnastics and medicine, which purge the body of ugliness and disease, respectively, and into punishment and instruction, which purge the soul of her wickedness and her ignorance, respectively. Instructional skills are said to be of two kinds, those concerned with technique and those concerned with the sort of education whose aim is the correction of those who think they know what they in fact do not know. This correction can take either of two forms. Those who think that ignorance is voluntary will often try to use skill in admonishing an offender, but those who think that all ignorance is involuntary will always try to refute the opinions of the offender so that he will become teachable.

Plato has the philosopher say that he is leery of calling an educator of the second type a sophist, but has him begrudgingly acknowledge the possibility that he might be defined in this way, since he does resemble the enlightened educator. But he warns Theaetetus that likenesses are slippery things and that a cautious man should be on his guard against them.

It may seem that the sixth definition is meant to classify the art practiced by Socrates and that the philosopher of the *Sophist* means to assign a noble lineage to it for this reason. However, Socrates' art is more encompassing than the art characterized here, which serves only the function of ridding the soul of the conceit of wisdom. In the *Theaetetus*, at 149A–151D, Socrates is made to liken his own art to that of midwifery and expresses the hope that through the practice of his art he will aid others in giving birth to wisdom. Part of this art, of course, is concerned with aborting false opinions, but no suggestion is made that these opinions must be dogmatically held. In the *Theaetetus*, for instance, Socrates practices his art on Theaetetus, who is not represented as presenting definitions of knowledge in a dogmatic fashion. It is also clear that Plato does not mean to be characterizing the art of the true philosopher, since dialectic includes use of the methods of collection and division and hypothesis, and it is taught only to students whose conceit of wisdom has already been purged. So it is likely that Plato simply means to call attention to the purgative value of the use made of the method of refutation by some sophists, (perhaps he is calling attention to Protagoras, for whom he usually shows respect,) and to register doubt about whether it is actually an attribute of the sophist.

In the *Gorgias*, at 464B–466A, Plato has Socrates say that there are two arts that aim at what is good for the body and two that aim at the good of the soul. The goods of the body are beauty and health, and the goods of the soul are knowledge and virtue. Gymnastics is said to be the art that purges the body of ugliness, and medicine the art that purges it of disease. It is implied that the legislative art is the art that purges the soul of ignorance, and that the judicial art is the art that purges her of wickedness. The ignorance purged by the art of the legislator would seem to be ignorance of how a life of virtue or excellence is led. The means by which this art accomplishes its task is to make laws that enable citizens of the state to know how to live virtuous lives. The judicial art, by contrast, would seem to purge the soul of wickedness by providing knowledge of how to judge those who fail to obey these laws. If this is correct, the sixth definition of the sophist is most likely not an attempt to characterize the legislative art. In the *Sophist* only the conceit of wisdom is purged by the alleged art of the sophist, while what seems to be purged by the legislative art is ignorance of how a virtuous life is led.

In the *Gorgias*, however, Socrates contrasts the four arts mentioned above with semblances of them. The first of these is cosmetology, which is a false image of gymnastics because it is not based on knowledge of beauty in the body and merely seems to purge the body of ugliness. The second he presents is the culinary art, which is a false image of medicine because it is not based on knowledge of health in the body and merely seems to purge the body of its disease by producing bodily pleasures. The third is sophistry, which Plato probably assumes to be a false image of the legislative art because it is not based on knowledge of how a virtuous life is led and merely seems to purge the soul of her ignorance of how to lead a life of virtue. The implication is that since a sophist claims to teach others how to be virtuous, he seems to be doing what a legislator is supposed to do. The fourth is rhetoric, which is a false image of the judicial art because it is not based on knowledge of virtue, and merely seems to purge the soul of her wickedness.

Although the point of Socrates' remarks in the *Gorgias* is to characterize rhetoric, we may extrapolate their point for the case of sophistry. Plato, I believe, is implying that a sophist, who claims to teach others how to lead virtuous lives, does not possess knowledge of how to lead such a life, and for this reason is only a false image of a legislator. In the *Sophist*, by contrast, the final definition of a sophist is that he is a false image of a wise man. These two characterizations, however, do not contradict one another, since in the *Gorgias* a definition of a sophist is not being put forward. A sophist indeed appears in many guises.

The final definition (232B–236D, 264D–268D)

Theaetetus now confesses that the many appearances of the sophist leave him at a loss about how to define his art. The philosopher says that a sophist, in turn, will be at a loss to know how to avoid a definition, because these very appearances are like the many grips of the wrestler that make it difficult for an opponent to escape. The implication is that a sophist is being held fast by each of the characterizations he has received and that he will finally be captured by a definition. The philosopher then summarizes the six appearances so they may more easily discern which among them provides a clue to the definition they seek. He says that although it seems that they have not yet identified the single skill by virtue of which a sophist receives his name, perhaps if they look among the skills attributed to him they may be able to see whether any one particularly appears to them to reveal his nature.

The philosopher claims that, from among the things they have said about a sophist, his characterization as a disputer about all things and as a teacher of disputation about all things seems especially to show what he is. It shows what a sophist is because the review of the six characterizations calls attention to the one skill *because of which* the other five are applicable to a sophist. Without his skill in disputation about all things, a sophist would not be successful in hunting young men, in selling them knowledge of virtue, and in refuting their opinions so that they will think it wise to receive instruction from him.

The philosopher then reminds Theaetetus that although a sophist pretends to have the knowledge to dispute about everything and to teach others to do so, he cannot actually possess such knowledge. How then, he asks, does a sophist manage to create the impression that he knows all things and get the young to pay money for instruction in disputation? The philosopher himself answers the question: a sophist is like an artist who is skilled at showing pictures of things to young children who are at a distance from the pictures in order to get them to believe that he can create the things pictured. Likewise, a sophist is skilled in the use of discourse to create images of truth in the souls of the young men who are at a distance from the truth in order to get them to believe that he speaks the truth. The philosopher adds that should the young men become acquainted with the truth, they will reject these semblances of the truth, just as the children reject the pictures as the things pictured when they become more mature. A sophist, he concludes, is a sort of magician or wonder-maker who entertains others by creating false images of the truth. He possesses, therefore, a kind of skill in making spoken false images of the truth.

Reflection on a sophist's claim to be able to dispute about everything has uncovered his appearance of possessing knowledge concerning all things, even though no one, including a philosopher, possesses knowledge of all things. That a philosopher is unlike a sophist in this respect is important, since it will help us to understand better in what way Plato believes that a sophist is a semblance of the wise man, while a philosopher is a likeness. A philosopher does not have, and does not profess to have, knowledge of all things because, although he has knowledge of the forms, he does not claim, as the infamous Protagoras does, for instance, to know the art of wrestling and all of the other special arts and sciences practiced in Athens. A sophist's skill in using disputation to make him appear wise in all things is a marvel in the way a painter's skill in deceiving children to think that his paintings of things are the things painted is a marvel. What Plato has in mind is that a painter's painting is related to what he has painted in the way a sophist's so-called wisdom is related to wisdom. The implication is that a sophist's so-called wisdom is not a likeness of wisdom, but only seems to be a likeness of it.

If we may assume that a philosopher's wisdom is in fact a likeness of the form, wisdom, then we may say that insofar as a sophist's so-called wisdom seems to be a likeness of this wisdom, but is not, he seems to be a philosopher, but is not. A sophist's so-called wisdom is like a shadow cast on the wall of the cave Plato uses in the *Republic* as part of a simile for the soul's progress from a state of perceptual judgment to a state of knowledge of the good. In the cave simile, a shadow is cast on this wall by a man-made image of a living thing that exists outside the cave. A sophist's so-called wisdom, he believes, is like a shadow of the philosopher's wisdom, which is a likeness of wisdom itself. In other words, just as a man-made image of a living thing is a likeness of a living thing outside the cave and the cave-wall image is a mere semblance, so a philosopher's wisdom is a likeness of wisdom itself and a sophist's so-called wisdom is a semblance.

A sophist manages to deceive the young to believe that he possesses the wisdom a philosopher in fact possesses, in spite of the fact that a philosopher does not claim to possess knowledge of all things. A sophist's skill in creating this belief lies in his ability to deceive the young that his spoken images of the truth express the truth, when in fact they do not. A philosopher's spoken images of the truth are his true statements, which are verbal expressions of true thoughts, which are likenesses of the truth. But a sophist's spoken images of the truth are his false statements, which are verbal expressions of false thoughts, which are semblances of the truth. It is these semblances of the truth that a sophist produces in the souls of the young. But the young, if brought up out of the cave, will see through a sophist's deceptions, since they will then have access to the truth. In the *Sophist*, Plato has the philosopher employ dialectic to enable Theaetetus to see through the sophist's deceptions.

Numerous examples of how a sophist deceives the young are presented in the *Euthydemus*, which is a dialogue in which Plato contrasts Socrates' use of argument with that of a sophist. Plato calls attention in this dialogue to the verbal tricks of a sophist. The first and perhaps the most commonly used trick is equivocation on terms, which enables a sophist to make it falsely appear that the conclusion of an argument is true because its premises are true. It was in part to avoid such specious reasoning that Socrates insisted that inquiry into the nature of things had to begin with definitions. The sophist is able to create the appearance of the conclusions of his arguments bring true because his opponents are ignorant of the equivocations employed in the arguments.

Another technique used by a sophist to deceive the young is to omit, either in a later premise of an argument or in the conclusion of an argument, a qualification explicitly or implicitly attached to a subject or predicate of a prior premise in the argument. An important example of this technique occurs in one of the arguments in the *Sophist*. In this argument, which will be explained later in this introduction, one of its true premises, which is that being, according to its own nature, is neither in motion nor at rest, is restated as the false premise that being is neither in motion nor rest. This unnoticed restatement of the premise makes it appear that it follows from the premise, that being, according to its own nature, is neither in motion nor at rest, that being cannot be made an object of discourse and thought, since what is neither in motion nor at rest cannot be made an object of discourse or thought. This false conclusion has been made to appear to follow from true premises, because the qualification, "according to its own nature," has been surreptitiously dropped from one of the premises. The ability of a sophist to make it appear as if a false conclusion follows from true premises ultimately led to the study of sophistic fallacies in argument. Aristotle, who taught in Plato's Academy, composed his *Sophistical Refutations* to expose such fallacies. It is very likely that Aristotle composed this work while he was in the Academy and used it as the basis of one of the courses he taught in logic.

There are two forms of skill in making images, the philosopher continues, since an image can be like its original or merely seem to be like its original. The first he calls skill in producing likenesses (*eikastikē*) and the second he calls skill in producing semblances (*phantastikē*). The skill in producing likenesses, he says, is possessed by the sculptor who can create, to the extent that his materials allow, an exact likeness of an object. Skill in producing semblances is possessed by a sculptor or painter who can create oversized images of his subject and compensate for distortions of perspective by changing the sizes of the parts near at hand so they do not appear too large and the parts farther away so they do not appear too small. The first skill enables one to make things be like their originals, and the second skill to make things that are not likenesses appear to be likenesses. Both of these skills are employed in the representational arts, which in *Republic* X are said to be concerned with imitating how things in the sensible world appear to us.

At this point the philosopher introduces an objection that a sophist would raise against the claim that he is creating semblances of the truth in the souls of the young and causing them to have false beliefs, and the dialogue turns to a consideration of this objection for the next twenty-eight Stephanus pages. The objection is interesting, not only because it enables Plato to introduce a problem he will solve in the dialogue, but also because it illustrates the sort of tricks in argument a sophist uses to make the young think that conclusions that are false follow from true premises.

After the objection has been answered, at 264B the philosopher returns to the task of defining a sophist. There he begins at the beginning, so to speak, by recalling the first division of art or skill introduced in the *Sophist*, the division into skill in producing things and skill in acquiring them. He does this so that he can place the image-making art into its proper genus. He divides the art of producing things into skills possessed by humans and those possessed by God, each of which, he believes, concerns either the production of things or the production of their images. Just as God, which Plato surely wants us to identify with the divine craftsman mentioned in the *Timaeus*, has skill both in creating the things of nature and in creating images of these, such as dream images, reflections in smooth bright surfaces, and even shadows, so also humans have skill in creating artifacts such as houses, and also skill in creating images of such artifacts and other things in nature.

Skill in making images, presumably both of the human and divine varieties, is divided into skill in making likenesses and skill in making semblances. A sophist possesses the latter sort of skill. Skill in making semblances of things are of two kinds, those in which an agent employs an external instrument in forming the image and those in which an agent himself serves as the instrument, as a sophist does in making himself appear to be wise by imitating the discourse of the wise. The philosopher says that this second skill, which he calls the art of imitation (*mimēsis*), can be utilized with knowledge of the true nature of the thing imitated or with only a belief about it, in which case it may be called belief-based imitation. Since a sophist, of course, does not have knowledge of the true nature of a wise man, he is a belief-based imitator.

A naïve belief-based imitator is one who thinks that he has knowledge of the true natures of the things he imitates, but since a sophist realizes that he lacks this knowledge, his skill in belief-based imitation is insincere. At this point the philosopher recalls a sophist's attribute of being a disputer and teacher of disputation, as opposed to being a speechwriter, like a demagogue. His skill in disputation, by virtue of which he is able to force others to say things that are contrary to one another, is the attribute he possesses by virtue of which he can make himself appear to be wise.

The dialogue ends with a statement of the definition of a sophist as a person who has the skill to imitate the wise, about whose true nature he has only a belief but pretends to have knowledge, by making others say things that are contrary to one another, his imitation being of the human form in which wondrous false images of the truth in discourse are produced.

PART TWO
THE OBJECTION OF A SOPHIST
(236C–264D)

The interpretation of *to mē on* and *ouk estin*

A clear understanding of Plato's account of how to use dialectic to answer a sophist's objection to a part of his final definition requires that I explain what I consider to be the correct translation of his use of *to mē on* and *ouk estin* in the dialogue. I do not, as most other scholars have, employ a contemporary linguistic or semantic framework to explain Plato's use of these terms, since I believe that to do so misrepresents what his account is. According to these contemporary linguistic frameworks, Plato's concern is to disambiguate uses or senses of "is not" (*ouk estin*) in negative statements, since the problem being discussed in the dialogue is whether what is not can be, where "what is not" is used as a translation of *to mē on.* This sort of disambiguation of *ouk estin*, however, I believe to be irrelevant to an understanding of the problem being discussed.

The sophist, we may say, objects to being classified as a dealer in images and falsehoods. His objection is that he cannot be a dealer in images and falsehoods because images and falsehoods cannot be. According to its standard linguistic and semantic interpretations, the objection is that images and falsehoods cannot be, since they can be only if what is not can be, but what is not cannot be, as Parmenides had argued in *On Nature*. Plato's reply, it is said, is to state that what is not can be, since it means "what is other than something that is," and what is other than something that is can be. Plato's reply to the objection is interpreted as the presentation of the theory that a negative statement, which expresses what is not, is reducible to a positive statement, which expresses that something is other than something that is. The problem with this interpretation is that it makes Plato's reply fail to be a proper answer to the objection. The reply would fail, even from Plato's own point of view, since in the *Sophist* a form is introduced for *to mē on*, which must be, on the standard view, a form for the negation of what is, and we know from Aristotle that Plato did not posit a form for a negation (*apophasis*).[16]

The standard interpretation does not take into account the fact that in Greek there is an ambiguity in the use of *to mē on* and the verbal construction, *ouk estin*, of which *to mē on* is the nominalization. The ambiguity to which I am calling attention, which cannot be reproduced in English, can be traced to the use of sentences of the form, "X *estin*," which in the *Sophist* Plato assumes to mean "X *on estin*," in which *on*, the neuter participle of *estin*, is being used as a noun, meaning "a being." A statement of this form, accordingly, is most accurately translated as "X is a being," rather than as "X is."

But if "X *estin*" means "X *on estin*," a statement of the form, "X *ouk estin*," can mean either "X *on ouk estin*" ("X is not a being") or "X *ouk on estin*" ("X is a non-being"). This ambiguity cannot be reproduced in English, which marks the difference by the use of "not" and "non-" in my translations of these different statement forms. Because Plato scholars have failed to see that there is this ambiguity in "X *ouk estin*," their translations of the *Sophist* into English usually (i) render *ouk estin* as "is not," which means "is not a being," rather than as "is a non-being," and (ii) render *to mē on* as "what is not," which means "not being" or "what is not a being," rather than as "non-being" or "a non-being." The translations employed by these other scholars, I contend, misrepresent both the sophist's objection to being classified as a dealer in falsehoods and images, and Plato's reply to the objection, since Plato is not concerned with the use of "is not" to deny being, but with the use of the predicate, "non-being," to refer to a being. In other words, his concern is not with statements of the form, "X *on ouk estin*," but with statements of the form, "X *ouk on estin*."

Although in the *Sophist* Plato is not analyzing statements of the form "X is not," he recognizes that "X *ouk estin*" is the form of a statement used in ordinary Greek to say that X is not a being. But an analysis of how it is used in ordinary Greek is not his concern in the *Sophist*. His concern is with Parmenides' use of a statement of this form in *On Nature*. As Parmenides used *ouk estin* in *On Nature*, according to Plato, it means *ouk on estin*, which Plato believes signifies participation in non-being rather than not participating in being. For this reason I do not believe that "X is not" is a suitable translation of "X *ouk estin*" in the *Sophist*.

Consequently, in this dialogue Plato does not deal with the problem of how it is possible, if something does not partake of being, it can be said to partake of being. Nor does he deal, as some scholars have claimed he does, with the problem of how to explain negative identity or negative predication statements expressed by the use of *ouk estin*. He is not reducing negative statements of existence, identity or predication expressed by the use of *ouk estin* to statements in which it is asserted that their subjects partake of non-being. In the *Sophist*, Plato is analyzing a statement in which non-being is predicated of a being; he argues that it does not mean that the contrary of being is predicated of a being, but that otherness in relation to something that is a being is predicated of a being. Since the contrary of being is the absence of being, Plato agrees that if non-being were the contrary of being, the predication of non-being of a being would be impossible.

How there can be many beings

Why would Plato interpret *to mē on* and *ouk estin* in this way if it is not the way in which they are used in ordinary Greek? I have already answered this question. It is because he thinks that it is the way in which Parmenides himself used them in *On Nature*. Although I believe that Plato has in fact correctly interpreted the use Parmenides makes of *to mē on* and *ouk estin* in *On Nature*,[17] I will not here set out my reasons for this belief, since it would require a careful explanation of what Parmenides says in *On Nature*, and my concern is with Plato's *Sophist*. I can, however, briefly explain why I think that Plato interprets Parmenides' use of the terms in this way.

When Parmenides argued that the appearance of the world being made up of many beings is false, Plato believes that Parmenides assumed that being and non-being are predicates of a subject and that being and non-being are contraries. Plato assumes that Parmenides argued that there cannot be many beings, since (i) there can be many beings only if being itself could be divided into many beings, each possessed by a different thing, (ii) only if there were a non-being that causes being to be divided in this way could it be so divided, but (iii) a non-being cannot be. Although in *On Nature*, Parmenides does not explicitly argue in just this way, Plato thinks that his argument can be analyzed somewhat in this way. So analyzed, Plato believes, the false premise of Parmenides' argument is that non-being cannot be. The only way in which this premise would be true, according to Plato, is if non-being is the absence of being, which is a predicate contrary to the predicate, being.

Why would Plato have thought that Parmenides assumed that being and non-being are contrary predicates of a subject? The answer, I believe, can be gleaned from the ancient reports that at one time Parmenides adopted a form of Pythagoreanism. If we assume that these reports are true, Parmenides was certainly familiar with the Pythagorean doctrine that the ultimate nature of all things is comprised of contrary principles and that from the combination of the most basic of these principles the world came to be made up of many things. The most basic of these principles they believed to be *peras* (being definite and with boundaries) and *apeiron* (being indefinite and without boundaries). Since one natural interpretation of these two principles is that they are, respectively, being and non-being, Plato might have thought that Parmenides meant to be rejecting a Pythagorean doctrine that beings are many because being and non-being, as contrary principles, are present in them.

In the *Sophist* itself, Plato's discussion of Parmenides' denial of the being of a non-being is not, except incidentally, an attempt to argue that there can be many beings because being combines with non-being. But his arguments for being combining with non-being, if sound, establish that there are many beings. His discussion of Parmenides' denial that non-being can be, however, is not meant to be an account of how many beings can be. His discussion of this denial occurs in the context of a sophist using the denial to avoid being classified as a dealer in images and falsehoods. Plato does, nonetheless, have the philosopher argue in the *Sophist* that Parmenides' view, that all things are one being, is incoherent.

That Plato believes that his account of non-being in the *Sophist* is the basis of a proper critique of Parmenides' argument against the possibility that there are many beings is supported by what Aristotle says in the *Metaphysics,* Book 14, Chapter 2. There Aristotle attributes to the Platonists the view that in order to demonstrate that there are many beings, it must be established, against Parmenides' claim, that a non-being cannot be, that a non-being can be.[18] Aristotle does not, in this chapter, explain Plato's account of what non-being is, since his concern is to show that it is false that all things other than non-being are non-beings by virtue of partaking of non-being. His argument against this view also targets Plato's view that all things other than being are beings by virtue of partaking of being. Aristotle argues that Plato's accounts of why there are many beings and non-beings is incoherent, since there is no one being or one non-being that causes things in the different categories of being to be beings or to be non-beings. Then he rejects the theory, which is expressed in the *Sophist*, that the forms possess elements (i.e. the greatest kinds). He argues that if the forms are composed of elements, they possess matter; but they cannot possess matter, since they are said to be eternal and what is eternal cannot possess matter.

Aristotle's clearest reference to the *Sophist* in this chapter is when he says that Plato and his followers were misled, when trying to explain why there are many beings, by Parmenides' primitive way of expressing the premise he used to deny that there can be many beings. This is the premise that a non-being cannot be. Aristotle says that the Platonists thought that they had to prove that a non-being can be in order to show that a plurality of beings is possible. It is clear that Aristotle is referring to the exposition of non-being as it is set out in the *Sophist*, since he explicitly says that "this thinker," who is obviously Plato, had in mind the problem of explaining falsehood when he presented his account of non-being.

The objection to the classification of a sophist (236D–237A)

As the philosopher is in the process of classifying a sophist as a person who has the verbal skill to make himself appear or seem to others to be wise and to say what is true when in fact he is not wise and what he says is not true, he stops to present an objection that a sophist would be likely to pose to this classification.[19]

> PHIL. My dear friend, we really are engaging in a very difficult inquiry. For this appearing to be or seeming to be without being, and saying things that are not true, all such things have always been and still are utterly perplexing. For it is very difficult, Theaetetus, to see how a person can say or believe that there really are falsehoods without being caught up in a statement that is contrary to itself.
> THEA. Why is it so difficult?
> PHIL. This statement is based on the daring hypothesis that a non-being is a being, since in no other way would a falsehood become a being (236D9–237A4)

Appearing to be and seeming to be are images of truth in the soul. Appearing to be and seeming to be without being are false images in the soul on the basis of which we make false perceptual judgments and hold false beliefs. These false images are created in our souls by the use of arguments that seem to establish the truth of their conclusions, but do not in fact do so. These images, however, are not themselves false beliefs or false perceptual judgments, which Plato identifies at 264A as conclusions of thought. They are the basis upon which false belief or false perceptual judgments rest.

The philosopher says that false images and statements are perplexing, but when in the next sentence he explains what the perplexity is, he mentions only what is perplexing about false statements. False statements, he believes, are spoken expressions of false beliefs and false perceptual judgments. The philosopher does not explain what the perplexity is about false images in the soul until 239D–240C, which concerns how images in general can be beings rather than how false images can be beings. The perplexity about falsehoods is further elucidated at 240C–241B. The falsehoods to which he refers in the passage just quoted are false statement, belief, and perceptual judgment.

Reference to a falsehood in the classification of a sophist is problematic, according to the above quotation, because a falsehood can be said or thought to be only if a non-being is a being, which is impossible. The philosopher does not explain why, if there is falsehood, a non-being is a being. That explanation is given at 240C–241B. When Plato has the philosopher say that the statement, that a non-being is a being, is "a statement that is contrary to itself" (*enantiologia*), he signals us the assumption upon which he believes that saying that a non-being is a being is "a daring hypothesis." He thinks that the sophist assumes that non-being is the contrary of being, and that for this reason, saying that a non-being is a being is to utter a statement in which it is assumed that contraries combine. The primary examples of contrary things cited by Plato in the *Sophist* are motion and rest. But if forms are contrary to one another, he thinks, neither can by itself combine with the other. He assumes that Parmenides' view is that since non-being is contrary to being, a non-being cannot be a being.

At 237A–239C, the philosopher presents Parmenides' warning to avoid saying and thinking that a non-being is a being and shows Theaetetus the difficulties Parmenides had in mind when he gave this warning. Then at 239C–240A the philosopher uses a sophistic argument to get Theaetetus to agree that these difficulties arise when an image is defined, and at 240A–242B he uses another sophistic argument to get Theaetetus to agree that these difficulties arise when a false belief or false statement is defined. After presenting these difficulties and sophistic arguments, at 241D–242A the philosopher announces that they will have to challenge Parmenides' maxim if the difficulties are to be overcome. The maxim is overturned later in the *Sophist* when the philosopher employs his skill in dialectic to prove that non-being is a being and that being is a non-being. So that we may be in a better position to understand the statements of the difficulties, the accounts of how an image and falsehood fall prey to these difficulties, as well as Plato's proofs that non-being is a being and that being is a non-being, here I will explain what I believe to be Plato's own theory of how and why we can think and speak of a non-being.

How and why we can speak and think of a non-being

The falsehoods to which Plato refers in the above quoted lines he interprets as false statements, false beliefs, and false perceptual judgments. The differences between these types of falsehoods need not concern us yet because what matters in the present context is that in all falsehoods things assumed to be beings are non-beings or things assumed to be non-beings are beings. Before we can understand how and why, if this is what a falsehood is, a non-being is said or thought to be, we need to understand why, if a non-being can be said or thought to be, non-being combines with being. Let us begin by examining closely how Plato himself seems to understand the meanings of statements of the forms "X *estin*" and "X *ouk estin*" as they are used by a sophist in the exposition of the natures of images and falsehoods.

Plato believes that to claim that an image or falsehood "is" (*estin*) means that it partakes of being. What does this belief entail for the interpretation of his use of "is" in this claim? Just as Plato will say that Socrates "is a man" (*anthrōpos estin*), if he partakes of [the] man (*ho anthrōpos*), or that the Parthenon "is beautiful" (*kalos estin*) if it partakes of the beautiful (*to kalon*), so, on this analogy, he should also say, as in fact he does, at 256D8–9, where he is explaining why motion is, that something "is a being" (*on estin*) because it partakes of [the] being (*to on*). In the light of these comparisons, Plato's own expansion of "is" to "is a being" in "motion is" implies that he uses "is" (*estin*) in such a claim as a copula that usually has an unexpressed predicate, "a being" (*on*). In general, Plato believes that "being" is a predicate in the sense that the term *on*, like *anthrōpos* and *kalon*, is a predicate attached to a subject by means of the copula, *estin*. Therefore, in the above cases, *estin* represents the participation of its subject in the form that by its own nature possesses the attribute signified by the predicate.[20]

From the perspective of the analysis of elemental discourse Plato presents in the *Sophist* itself, *estin* is a verb, when used by itself, without an explicit object, in a sentence, is comparable to "sits" (*kathetai*) or "flies" (*petetai*), when applied to Theaetetus. What is signified in each case is participation in the form that by its own nature possesses the attribute signified by the participial version of the verb in English. When *estin* is by itself coupled with a noun or pronoun in the subject position of a sentence, it means "is a being." When *estin* is applied to a subject other than being, it signifies participation in the form of being, just as "sits" and "flies" signify participation in the forms of sitting and flying when Theaetetus is said to sit or to fly.

To be a being, according to Plato, is not to be something of a certain kind or to possess an attribute. To be something of a certain kind or to possess an attribute, he thinks is to be something (*ti*). Plato seems to think, for reasons I will cite below, that to be a being is to possess causal power. If this is in fact what he believes, and he surely does, he thinks, for instance, that forms are beings because they can cause thoughts in the soul, thoughts are beings because they can caused to be in the soul, the soul is a being because it can cause bodily motion, bodily motion is a being because it be caused by the soul, etc. But horned rabbits and unmarried bachelors, he would say, are not beings, since they cannot causally interact with anything else.

Nor is the form of being the form by participation in which "is" can be attached to a subject. It is the form by participation in which "being" (*on*) can be attached to a subject other than being itself by means of "is" (*estin*). Plato believes that the form, being, is that which possesses causal power by its own nature and causes whatever partakes of it to possess causal power.

From Plato's perspective, Parmenides claimed that when philosophers in Greece attempted to explain how the many things that appear to our senses and minds come to be, they committed themselves to the unintelligible view that non-beings are beings. Plato also thinks that Parmenides challenged the early Greek philosophers' assumption that there can be more than one being, since being cannot be many unless caused to be so by combining with non-being, which cannot be. Parmenides therefore warned these philosophers:

> "Never let it prevail that non-beings are beings.
> In pursuit of the truth keep your thought from this path."

In the *Sophist* Plato takes up the task of showing that non-beings are beings. But he does not do so for the purpose of explaining how a being can come to be or how there can be many beings. In the *Sophist* he argues that non-beings can be beings in order to answer an objection a sophist would bring to the claim images and falsehoods can be.

In Plato's *Timaeus*, it is said that forms or ideas are exemplars used by the divine mind (*nous*) for the creation of sensible changing things in the receptacle. Although the details of how this mind accomplishes its task are not clear, Plato does tells us in the *Timaeus* that this mind "persuades necessity" to bring order into the disorderly motions in the receptacle whose being he believes must be posited in order to provide a place for images of the forms.[21] Part of the order introduced into the motions in the receptacle is their arrangement into patterns that are, in some mysterious way, likenesses of the forms.[22] Although they are like the forms, sensible changing things do not possess by themselves the natures of the forms they are like. However, since sensible things are made to be like the forms and we were acquainted with the forms before we entered bodies, we recollect the forms when we perceive their sensible likenesses. These recollections appear in our souls as conceptual images of attributes that are predicated of the forms by their own natures. Plato most likely believes that we are capable of recollecting the forms because in our souls[23] is a divine part, an immortal intellective soul, which enables us to recollect the forms in this way because it is always directly aware of them.[24]

In a statement whose subject is represented as partaking of a form, a name assigned to the subject is combined either (i) with a verb that signifies the subject partaking of a form, or (ii) with the copula, "is," along with the name or implied name of an attribute of a form. The name assigned to the subject may or may not be the name of a form. Examples of names assigned to the subject and that are not names of forms are (i) pronouns such as "this," "he, "it," etc., as in "This is a man" and "He is a man," or the name of the form itself, along with a demonstrative pronoun, as in "This man is an animal," or (ii) a proper name of a sensible object, along with the assumption that this object partakes of some form or other, as in "Socrates is a man" and "Socrates is an animal."

If one form is said to partake of a second, each is then said to be combined with the other. If one form is said to partake of a second, the second is then said to possess the attribute that belongs to the first by its own nature. The first, however, does not possess that attribute by its own nature, but only because it partakes of the first. Each form is capable of being combined with certain others, and some forms are capable of being combined with all others. The divine mind conceives the attribute that belongs to a form by its own nature, conceives which forms can and which cannot combine, and combines forms those combination serves the good. Hence, some forms that are not contrary to one another are combined, while others are not.

The philosopher in the *Sophist* first calls attention to three of the greatest kinds, which he calls "being" (*to on*), "motion" (*kinēsis*) and "rest" (*stasis*). They are the greatest kinds by virtue of each being a form of which everything other than itself combines. It has sometimes been thought peculiar that Plato should think that everything other than rest combines with rest, since Plato himself believes that motion, which is contrary to rest, does not combine with rest. How then can everything other than rest combine with rest if motion cannot combine with rest?

In the *Sophist,* being is defined as active or passive causal powers. If we assume that Plato believes this to be the correct definition of being, it is likely that he defines motion as the exercise of an active or passive causal power and defines rest as the non-exercise of an active or passive causal power. Again, in the *Sophist* the philosopher is made to say that something can combine with being either by itself or in relation to something else. For instance, Theaetetus combines with being by himself, while sitting combines with being in relation to Theaetetus if Theaetetus is sitting. If we assume that Plato himself believes that something can combine with being either by itself or in relation to something else, it is also likely that he believes that something can combine with rest or with motion either by itself or in relation to something else.

We can now explain how everything other than rest, including motion, combines with rest, since even though motion cannot combine with rest by itself, it can combine with rest in relation to something else. For instance, motion combines with rest in relation to a form that does not combine with motion, since motion is not exercising a causal power to be combined with another form in relation to that form. Although it is true that a causal power cannot both be and not be exercised at the same time in relation to the same thing, something can possess a causal power that is being exercised in relation to one thing but not being exercised in relation to another. In this way, one thing can possess a causal power that both is and is not being exercised, albeit in relation to different things. One thing may also possess different active and passive powers, some of which are being exercised and the others not.

In the process of explaining how being, motion and rest are related, the philosopher introduces two more of the greatest kinds, which he calls "the same" (*tauton*) and "the other" (*thateron*). The same, we may assume, is the form that, when one thing partakes of it, this thing is the same as itself, and when two things partake of it, they are the same as one another. To be the same, in each case, is to be the same in number. The other is the form that by partaking of which something is other in number than something else. The other is not the form by participation in which something is other in kind than something else, since Plato's examples include not only cases in which, for instance, motion is other than being, but also cases in which one being is other than another. There is, moreover, no reason to suppose that he confused being other in kind with being other in number. When the philosopher is made to claim that being, motion and rest are other than one another, for instance, he means that they are other in number than one another rather than that they are other in kind. In any case, in his view, forms that are other in kind are also other in number. At a later point in the *Sophist* he argues that non-being is the form by participation in which something is other than a being to which it is set in contrast. In this case, the two beings that are set in contrast are other than one another in number.

In the statement that non-beings are beings, which is implicitly universal in scope, the plural form of the name of the nature of non-being is joined, as above, by the copula, with the plural form of the name of the nature of being. The statement means that non-being and the things that partake of non-being are beings. In Plato's view, unless the form, non-being, is a being, there could be no being by partaking of which anything else would be a non-being, and hence there could be no non-beings in this sense. So if a non-being is a being, non-being itself must partake of being. And since if one form partakes of another, they combine, then if non-being itself is a being, non-being must combine with being. But this is impossible if non-being is contrary to being. In 237B–239B Plato has the philosopher explain the difficulties created by the assumption that non-being is contrary to being. Since the difficulties are set out as an explanation of the problems that Parmenides thinks we face if "we speak of a non-being" (237B), it is clear that Plato believes that Parmenides assumed in *On Nature* that non-being is the contrary of being.

The objection to non-being (237B–239C)

The philosopher is now made to present a number of difficulties created when reference is made to non-beings. I will refer to these difficulties collectively as the objection to non-being. After the philosopher quotes Parmenides' warning not to say or think that there are non-beings, he explains why the warning was made. The explanation takes the form of showing what the difficulties are that are faced by someone who would try to use discourse or thought to make reference to non-beings. These difficulties will arise in attempts to explain how there can be images and falsehoods. At 237B–239C Plato presents three such difficulties, each purportedly worse than its predecessor.

The first, presented at 237B–E, is that a non-being cannot be given a name, since only beings possess a character and a unity by virtue of which they can be named, and a non-being cannot be a being. Plato begins the argument by asking to what the name, *to mēdamōs on*, could be applied. The use of *mēdamōs* in place of *mē* in the earlier *to mē on* is a device Plato employs to signal the reader that *mē* was meant to signify contrariety to the nature of being. In the translation and hereafter I will indicate the strengthening of the negative prefix by italicizing "non-."

We may now say that he begins his statement of the first difficulty of speaking or thinking of a non-being by asking to what the expression, "*a non*-being" can be applied. He then has Theaetetus agree that

(1) "Non-being" should not be applied to any being.

This statement, as I said above, is based on the assumption that non-being is contrary to being. The next statement in the argument assumes that being itself is a being, and hence, that "non-being" should not be applied to being itself.

He continues, therefore, by claiming that

> (2) If "non-being" should not be applied to a being, it should not be applied to something (*to ti*, 237C10), since we always use "something" to refer to a being.

The something to which "non-being" should not be applied is a thing of a certain kind. In better English, we would say that it should not be applied to anything, but I have retained "something" because this is a more exact translation of the Greek word, *ti*. The use of the definite article, *to*, before *ti* is to call attention to the specific word used to refer to something of some kind. The philosopher is surely not saying that "non-being" should not be applied to the *word*, *ti*. That to which this word is applied, in the first instance, is the form whose nature is signified by the word. What the word, *ti*, signifies is a thing of a certain kind. Plato believes, it seems, that there is a form by virtue of which all things that partake of it are things of a certain kind. (To partake of a form, consequently, is not to be a thing of a certain kind.) The philosopher adds:

> (3) "Something" in the singular form is a sign of one thing, in the dual, a sign of a pair of things, and in the plural, a sign of many things.

The philosopher goes on to assume that if "something" in the singular is a sign of one thing, then since the expression formed by placing the negative sign before it will not be a sign of a pair of things or many things, it must be a sign of what is not one in any way. Premise (3) is included in this argument so that attention is called to the use of "something" to refer to what is one. His is done in order to justify, in the next premise, the substitution of "non-one" for "non-something." Consequently,

> (4) It follows necessarily that he who speaks of non-something (*mē ti*) is speaking of *non*-one (*pantapasi mēden*).

Here and in (5) below to speak of something means to use a name to refer to it, since in (1) and (2) it is the application of a name to something that is in question.

The translation of (4) needs to be explained. In other contexts *pantapasi mēden,* translated here as "*non*-one," would be translated for reasons of good English prose as "nothing at all," even though, from an etymological point of view, it literally means "no one thing at all." Most other translators, in fact, translate it here as "nothing at all." But the idea of nothing is that of not being a thing of any kind at all and is already captured in this premise by *mē ti*, which I have, to retain the course of the argument, rendered as "non-something." In this part of the argument the philosopher is assuming that since a thing being something and being one are equivalent, "non-one" can be substituted for "non-something" in the argument. Although to understand (4) we need to realize that in Greek to say that something is *mēden* is the English equivalent to saying that something is nothing, (4) cannot be translated into the English equivalent without obscuring what the argument is.

Finally, it is assumed that since (i) one who speaks of non-one (we can mentally substitute for "non-one" here the term "nothing") does not speak at all, (ii) one who speaks of non-one speaks of non-something, and (iii) one who speaks of non-something speaks of non-being, it follows that

(5) In trying to speak of a non-being one is not speaking at all.

In other words, to use a name to refer to a non-being is not to use a name at all, since nothing is named and a name is what refers to something.

The second difficulty of speaking or thinking of a non-being upon which Parmenides' warning is based is presented at 238A–C. The difficulty is that since what partakes of the one or partakes of the many is a being, and so cannot be combined with non-being, we cannot use speech or thought to make reference to a non-being, for all such reference and expression require a non-being to be one or many. It is here claimed that what is one being or many beings cannot be combined with non-being because it is assumed that non-being is contrary to being. This difficulty is considered worse than the first because it shows that it will be impossible not only to refer to a non-being, but also impossible to saying anything about it. The third and worst difficulty, which is presented as 238D1–239C8, is that since the statements of the first two difficulties make reference to and speak about a non-being, they too encounter those difficulties, and so should be abandoned.

Plato calls attention to the assumption that non-being is contrary to being when he has the philosopher conclude that he and Theaetetus have been forced to speak of that which is contrary to itself (*enantia auton autōi peri ekeino anagkadsesthai legein*, 238D6–7), since they have been forced to say that a being is a non-being. Non-being, Plato has the philosopher remark, would seem to have provided a place for the sophist to hide, since the attempt to classify him would require that these difficulties be faced.

To side-step these difficulties, Plato believes, the philosopher needs to expose and overturn Parmenides' assumption that the non-being is contrary to being. If we make this assumption, Plato agrees, reference to non-beings are in fact problematic. In fact, he has the philosopher say as much at 258D–259A. The philosopher says

> Let no one say to us that we are showing non-being to be contrary to being when we dare to say that it is a being. For we long ago said goodbye to any contrary to being, whether it is or is not a being and has an account or has no account at all.

The philosopher says goodbye to any contrary to being here at 237B-239B, where it has been shown that if non-being is contrary to being, non-being is unnamable and unthinkable. This does not mean that Plato thinks that we cannot deny that something is a being; it means that we cannot predicate the contrary of being of a being, since there is no contrary of being. To say that something does not partake of being, according to Plato, is not to say that something partakes of the contrary of being. If something could partake of the contrary of being, Plato believes, there would be a form for the contrary of being, and there is none. Nor is there a form for not partaking of being.[25]

At 239C–241C, the philosopher employs the tricks of a sophist to get Theaetetus to agree that when we give an account of images or an account of falsehoods, we are forced to make statements that are contrary to themselves, where statements contrary to themselves are statements in which contrary predicates are applied to a subject. He first argues, at 239C–240C, that an explanation of what an image is forces us to say of a being that it is a non-being, and then he argues, at 240C–241C, that an explanation of what a falsehood is forces us to say of a being that it is a non-being. These arguments, of course, are presented on behalf of a sophist, who relies upon the assumption that non-being is contrary to being.

How the difficulties arise for the account of an image (239C–240C)

At 240A–B, the philosopher, who is assuming the role of a sophist, has his student, Theaetetus, agree that

> (1) An image is something that is made to be like another thing that is real.

When the philosopher asks Theaetetus whether an image is like the other thing in being real, Theaetetus says that it is a likeness of a real thing, but

> (2) An image is not at all a real thing.

What Theaetetus should have said, of course, is that an image is not at all a real thing it is like, not that the image is not at all a real thing. This is a slip made by Theaetetus that will allow the philosopher, who is playing the part of a sophist in this exchange, to change the meaning of what Theaetetus meant to say. Ordinarily, it is a sophist who fails to add the qualification to the denial that something is true of a subject, not the person he is trying to get to say something that is contrary to itself. This is the sort of trick of argument used by a sophist that Socrates is made to parody in the *Euthydemus.* Here in the *Sophist* Plato very cleverly has Theaetetus make a statement in which the qualification is dropped in order to show his reader that a sophist can also take advantage of our own failure to add the necessary qualification to what we assert or deny of a subject.

By having Theaetetus state (2) as an explanation of the difference between an image and what it represents, Plato illustrates how the inexperience of the young enables a sophist to get him to contradict himself. Theaetetus' lack of experience in argument will enable the philosopher in a later premise of the argument to conclude, from an image being "not at all a real thing" that it is "not really a being."

So the argument continues with Theaetetus seeming to have committed himself to saying that

(3) A real thing really is a being.

This premise is simply a definition of what a real thing is. Then Theaetetus is made to say that

(4) A non-real thing is contrary to a real thing.

Theaetetus is led to accept (4) on the basis of (3) and the assumption that the difficulties of talking about a non-being were based on the contrariety of a non-being and a being. If a real thing really is a being, a non-real thing really is a non-being, and being and non-being are contraries, it seems to follow that a non-real thing is contrary to a real thing. Therefore, it seems, since an image is not at all a real thing, and a real thing is really a being, it seems to follow, Theaetetus agrees, that:

(5) An image is really a non-being.

In (5) I have substituted "image" for "likeness," which occurs in the text, so that the logic of the argument of which (5) is a part is transparent. More significant is my rendering of the phrase, *ontōs ouk estin* as "is really a non-being." I take the implicit form of this phrase to be *ontōs ouk on estin* in which *ouk* modifies *on,* rather than, *ontōs on ouk estin*, in which *ouk* modifies *estin*, which would be translated as "really is not a being." The point then, is that Theaetetus is committed to predicating non-being of an image, which means, he thinks, that the difficulties of predicating non-being of something arise when an account of an image is presented.

In the text itself the philosopher adds to (5) the rider, "when you say that it is a non-real thing," but this addition, as far as the logic of the argument is concerned, simply emphasizes the use of premise (2) in the derivation of (5). The use of the rider, however, is an important part of the sophistic trick of getting Theaetetus to recall premise (2) in the form in which it does, along with (3) and (4), entail (5), while ignoring (1) which was the basis upon which (2), in its loose form, is asserted. The conclusion drawn, of course, is that if a sophist is to be classified as image-maker, the difficulty created by the acceptance of Parmenides' maxim must be faced. The remainder of this exchange between the philosopher and Theaetetus simply calls attention to the problematic character of (5). Theaetetus protests that an image is in some way a being, even if not in the way a real thing is a being. It is concluded that if we explain what an image is, we must in speech or thought refer to a non-being.

How the difficulties arise for the account of false belief (240D–241C)

How a sophist would object to being classified as a dealer in falsehoods is introduced at 240D. An accurate rendition of the objection into English requires an awkward English translation. For instance, I represent the philosopher as defining false belief as "believing that things contrary to beings are beings" (*t'anantia tois ousi doxadsousa*). The things in question are things believed to be beings in relation to the subject of the belief. For instance, when it is believed that Theaetetus flies, what is believed to be a being is flying. In this case, flying, which is a non-being in relation to Theaetetus, is falsely believed to be a being in relation to Theaetetus.

The definition of false belief as believing that things contrary to beings are being is quickly paraphrased by the philosopher as the definition that false belief is "believing that non-beings are beings" (*to mē onta doxadsousa*), apparently to reinforce Theaetetus' identification of things contrary to beings with non-beings. Theaetetus, I assume, realizes that believing that non-beings are beings means that believing that non-being in relation to a subject are beings in relation to a subject.

The philosopher concludes that in their attempts to characterize what an image is and what a falsehood is they have combined being and non-being. So the philosopher decides, at 241C–242B, that if they are to resolve the difficulty posed by the classification of a sophist as a dealer in false images and falsehoods, they must refute Parmenides' maxim by arguing that (i) there is a sense in which non-being is a being (*to te mē on hōs esti kata ti*, 241D6–7) and that (ii) there is a sense in which being is a non-being (*to on au palin hōs ouk esti pei*, 241D7). At 255E–257A, an argument for (ii) is presented, and at 257B–258C and an argument for (i) is presented. In the process, it will also be shown that non-being is not contrary to being.

Why being is other than other beings (242B–249D)

Plato believes that a refutation of the view, that a non-being is not a being, requires that the philosopher show that being is other than everything that is a being by virtue of partaking of being. So he has the philosopher set out to establish that being is other than these others by calling attention to errors about being that his predecessors committed when they attempted to set out the number of beings there are and the nature of being. The error Plato believes his predecessors committed concerning the number of the most elemental beings there are is that they failed to include, when they counted the number of elemental beings there are, the form by participation in which they are beings. The error he believes his predecessors committed concerning the nature of being is that they identified the nature of being with the natures of things that partake of being. He has the philosopher argue that the form of being is other than the beings that partake of it so that the philosopher can go on to argue that things other than the form of being are non-beings in the sense that they are other than this being and that the form of being is a non-being because it is a being other than any being that partakes of it. He also has the philosopher argue that there is a form by participation in which they are non-beings in this way and that the nature of this form is to be other than something that is a being.

Some of the philosophers who discussed how many elemental beings there are, the philosopher says, claimed that there are many, others that there is just one, and yet others that they are both many and one. To what extent these philosophers meant to delineate the exact number of beings there are is not clear, but we can be sure that Plato has the philosopher interpret them in this way so that he might relate what they did say to his own account of being.

Those who attempted to determine the number of beings there are we may call the pluralists and the monists. The pluralists are those who claimed that sensible changing objects are beings just insofar as they are composed of a number of contrary-natured elemental beings. The monists are those who hold opposing view, that there is just one being.

It is not clear who the pluralists are who hold the view that there are just two contrary-natured elemental beings. Aristotle does not mention this view when, in the first book of the *Metaphysics*, he discusses his predecessors' views concerning the elements of all changing sensible objects. The pair of elemental beings the philosopher mentions are the wet and/or hot and the dry and/or cold. The view that the contrary-natured elemental beings are three in number may be that of Pherecydes, the surviving fragments of whose poem would indicate that he posited three. Two of these, Zas and Cthonie, possess natures contrary to one another and cause the sensible objects in which they are present to possess contrary attributes, and the third, Chronus or Time, would seem to be the cause of the continued being of the sensible objects in which it is present in spite of their possession of contrary attributes. According to both versions of the views held by the pluralists, the being of each and every changing sensible object must be many rather than one, since all sensible objects must possess contrary attributes in order to continue to be the same beings through change of contrary attributes.

The monists, of course, are the Eleatics. Their view is expressed as the view that "all things are one being." The things, all of which are one being, are the subjects of discourse and thought. Plato assumes that the Eleatics believe (i) that if the subjects of discourse and thought are beings, their being is caused by the presence in them of being, (ii) that if the subjects of discourse and thought are different beings, each being a different being is caused by something that causes being to be dispersed among them, (iii) that this thing, since other than being, is a non-being, (iv) that a non-being cannot be, and so (v) that the subjects of discourse and thought cannot be different beings. The Eleatics concluded, therefore, that all subjects of discourse and thought are one being. Consequently, the appearance of the subjects of discourse and thought being many different beings is illusory. The Eleatics also believed, of course, that if the subject of discourse and thought is a being, it cannot come to be a being or cease to be a being, since it would need to come to be from its non-being or pass away into its non-being, and a non-being cannot be.

The philosopher includes in a third category the theories of Heraclitus and his followers and of Empedocles and his followers, according to whom "being is both one and many." Strictly speaking, these thinkers do not ascribe either to the view of the pluralists, who deny that all sensible changing objects can be one, or the view of the monists, who deny that being can be many. Let us call this view the non-contrariety view of the number of being, because it implies that the one and the many are not contraries, and so, can combine.[26] Although the philosopher attributes the non-contrariety view of the number of being to both of these philosophical schools of thought, he makes it clear that it does not have the same meaning for both.

The Heracliteans, according to this interpretation of their view of the number of being, understand being to be both one and many at the same time. It is many because every being, which for them is a changing sensible object, possesses contrary attributes, but one insofar as the contrary attributes it possesses are held fast together by enmity.[27] In the *Theaetetus* Plato says that the Heracliteans denied that the things we sense possess fixed natures of their own by virtue of which each is one thing by itself.[28] A sensible object can possess contrary attributes precisely because it is not, apart from the binding action of enmity, one thing.

Aristotle also tells us, in *Metaphysics* IV, that the Heracliteans accepted the view that sensible objects possess contrary attributes. He believes, as Plato does, that this view led to Protagoras' doctrine that man is the measure of all things. In the *Theaetetus,* Plato argues that the Heracliteans' view, that all sensible things are constantly changing both in place and in quality, fails to provide a metaphysical foundation upon which names can be assigned to them. If sensible objects, he argues, cannot in some way remain one thing over time, they cannot be named or conceived, and so, cannot even be said or thought to be constantly changing. Plato himself, of course, believes that the way in which sensible objects remain one thing over time, in spite of lacking fixed natures of their own by virtue of which they are one thing, is by continuing to be reproduced in the receptacle as images of one and the same form.

The Empedocleans think that the being of sensible changing things becomes one at the time when cosmic friendship prevails in the world and many at the time when cosmic strife prevails. Nonetheless, they believe, the being of the world is comprised of the four basic contrary-natured elements, called earth, fire, air, and water, and for this reason are four distinct beings. When, by the power of cosmic friendship, all of these elements properly combine, they somehow cease to be distinct beings. But this one being itself is caused, by the power of cosmic strife, to pass away into the many elemental beings from which it came to be.

This Empedoclean view, according to Plato, does not, any more than does the Heraclitean view, adequately deal with the problems of how sensible objects can be many different beings and how beings can come to be and pass away, since neither addresses the problem of how non-beings can be beings. The Heracliteans and the Empedocleans do not seem to have realized, Plato believes, that there can only be one cause of the being of sensible objects: the participation of each in being. Nor does he think that they realize that there can only be one cause of these beings being different beings at different times, which is their participation in non-being.

The philosopher argues, at 243D–244B, that the pluralists were unclear about what is signified by "is a being" when they said that each of their elements is a being by itself. Although he does not say so explicitly, the philosopher means that the pluralists did not ask themselves why these elements are called beings. He believes that they failed to inquire about what the cause is of their possession of being, since without a statement of that cause, their account of what beings there are is in complete.

If we ask those who posit a pair of elemental being whether the cause of their being is itself another being, he says, they cannot say that it is, since they have not listed it among the elemental beings. Nor can they say that it is the same as either one of the elemental beings they specify or the same as both together. Should they say that the cause of their possession of being is the same as just one of their elements, they could not call the other a being. The unstated reason is that one cannot cause the other to be a being by combining with it. One can combine with the other, since they possess contrary natures. Should they say that the cause of the being of other things is the same as both of these elements together, they would be saying that a pair of elemental beings that possess contrary natures comprises one being. We are to infer that if the pluralists were clear that their elemental beings require a third being to cause their possession of being, they would adjust their enumeration of elemental beings accordingly.

The philosopher next calls attention, at 244B–245E, to the difficulties that arise for the monists because they are unclear about what is signified by "being" in "is a being." Plato thinks that the view, that there is just one being, is incoherent, since it is both one and a being, and so it is many. The full form of the theory of the monists, according to Plato, is as follows:

> (1) If there are many beings, all are beings by reason of the presence in them of being itself.
> (2) If things are non-beings, non-being combines with being.
> (3) But non-being cannot combine with being.
> (4) If things are not non-beings, all things are one being.
>
> Therefore,
> (5) All things are one being.
> (6) If all things are one being, there is only one being.
>
> Therefore,
> (7) There is only one being.
> (8) The one being all things are is a whole of parts.

Of these, the philosopher has no objection to (1), (2), (4) or (6), and his criticism of (3) is reserved for his solution to the PNB. Here he targets (5), (7) and (8). He presents three different objections to them.

The first objection is that the one being that all things are is not one. The philosopher argues that if being is said to be one, it is called by two names, "being" and "one." But then, contrary to (5) and (7), there are two beings and not all things are one being. Moreover, if being itself has any name at all, then contrary to (7), there will be two beings, being itself and its name, and contrary to (5), not all things are one being. Then he adds that the name of being cannot be the same as being itself, since it will be the name of nothing or name itself, both of which are absurd.

The second objection is that it cannot be true *both* that the one being is a whole of parts *and* that all things are one being. He argues that if the one being is a whole of parts, it is one in relation to its parts. But if it is one in relation to its parts, it is not the one, which is the form by partaking of which it is one, since this one is partless. He adds that if it is not the one itself, then contrary to (7), there will be two beings, the one being that has parts, and the one, which does not, in which case, contrary to (5), not all things will be one being. So either the one being all things are is not a whole of parts, contrary to (8), or not all things are one being, contrary to (7).

The third objection is that the one being cannot be a whole of parts. This objection, however, is stated in a very elliptical way because it is designed to counter an effort to avoid the second objection. The dilemma just presented turns on the assumption that the one being is a whole because it is one in relation to its parts, and so partakes of the one. It might be thought, therefore, that thesis (8) can be saved if we suppose that the one being is a whole because it partakes of the whole. The philosopher argues that this move will not work, since if the one being is a whole of parts, not by partaking of the one, but by partaking of the whole, the whole of which it is said to partake is either a being or a non-being. First he argues that the whole cannot be a being and then that the whole cannot be a non-being.

The argument for the conclusion that the whole cannot be a being begins with the statement that if the whole, by partaking of which being is a whole of parts, is a being, being will fall short of itself. The sense in which it will fall short of itself seems to be that it will not be a being, since the whole is a being and there is only one being. But if being is not a being, it is, contrary to (3), a non-being. But if it is not the case that being is not a being, and the whole too is a being, there will be, contrary to (7), more than one being.

The argument for the conclusion that the whole cannot be a non-being begins with the statement that if the whole, by partaking of which being is a whole of parts, is a non-being, being will again fall short of itself in the sense that it will not be a being. Moreover, if being is not a being, it is a non-being, which contradicts (3). Moreover, if the whole, by partaking of which being is a whole of parts, is a non-being, a being cannot come to be, since what comes to be must come to be a whole of parts, and a being cannot be a whole of parts if the whole is a non-being. And if a being cannot come to be, what comes to be cannot be said to be a being.

Finally, he argues that if the whole, by partaking of which being is a whole of parts, is a non-being, being must be a non-whole, since there is no whole by partaking of which it is a whole of parts, and if being is a non-whole, it cannot be of any quantity, since only a whole of parts is of some quantity. But if the whole cannot be a being or a non-being, the philosopher implies, then the one being cannot be a whole of parts by partaking of the whole, and the second objection cannot be successfully avoided by the claim that the one being is a whole by partaking of the whole rather than by partaking of the one. The upshot of Plato's critique of the theories of the number of being is that the pluralists and the monists have not realized that the being they have attributed to the many and the one is other than the many and the one.

After Plato has the philosopher lead Theaetetus through this critique of the views of the pluralists and monists concerning the number of beings, we might have expected him to include an appraisal of the non-contrariety view, but none is presented. Why the appraisal is excluded is not explained. However, he probably thinks that this view is subject to the same basic fault as the view of the pluralists. It would surely have said that it omits being itself as a being, and being itself does not come to be or pass away. For Plato, only the motions of the stuff in the receptacle that partakes of the forms can come to be and pass away. A subject of discourse or thought is either a being by its own nature or a being by virtue of partaking of that which is a being by its own nature.

At 245E–249D the philosopher divides those who contend with one another about the nature of being into those who believe that to be a being is to be a body and those who believe that it is to be a form, and then he examines their views individually. His intent is to show that those who propound these views fail to realize that being is a third thing, a form by participation in which both bodies and forms are beings. Those who hold the first view he calls the giants and those who hold the second he calls both the gods and the friends of the forms. Those who hold the first view I will call the materialists and those who hold the second, the immaterialists. The materialists, most scholars of Plato's philosophy believe, are the atomists. They do not agree, however, about who the immaterialists are. Although the philosopher calls them friends of the forms, and they do in fact hold, as Plato does, that there is a world of mind and its ideas, they do not think, as Plato does, that bodies are beings. Whoever the immaterialists are, it is certain that the view presented on their behalf here is not that of Plato; for he neither identifies being with form nor denies that bodies and their motions are beings.

Although, as Aristotle tells us, the atomists identified non-being with the void, this part of their theory, if it is counted as part of the philosophy of the materialists, is not mentioned because it is irrelevant to the point the philosopher wants to make about their use of "is a being." Other relevant parts of the theory of the materialists the philosopher does not explicate until after he introduces the theory of the immaterialists, one of whose theses is the rejection of the view that to be a being is to be a body.

The main thesis of the immaterialists' theory is that to be a being is to be a form. The philosopher has them say that forms are "objects of the mind" (*noēta)* and without bodies (*asōmata)*, but the intent of this characterization of their view is to make it clear why they reject the main thesis of the materialists.

The philosopher seems to be alluding to the atomism of the materialists when he says that the immaterialists shatter the bodies of their opponents "into small pieces in their arguments." He means, presumably, that their arguments do to the atomism of the materialists what they themselves do to the bodies with which they identify being. That is to say, they break the atoms into smaller parts, which probably means that the immaterialists use arguments to reject the atomism of the materialists.

The materialists, the philosopher adds, ascribe to bodies a continuous coming to be that the immaterialists believe to be contrary to their being. The atomists, of course, do analyze the bodies we sense into collections of atoms and claim that these atoms are in constant motion in the void. That they also claim that the bodies they divide into collections of atoms are always coming to be is clear enough, since they believe that the collections of atoms of which they are composed are constantly changing due to the constant motion of their atoms. If we incorporate this information into the last part of the philosopher's account of the immaterialists' characterization of their opponents' theory, we may unpack it, I believe, as the argument that since bodies are composed of atoms, atoms are always in motion; but if atoms are always in motion, the bodies of which they are composed are always coming to be; so the bodies of which atoms are composed are always coming to be. The immaterialists add that what always comes to be and being are contraries. So the immaterialists infer both that what always comes to be is not a being and that bodies are not beings. At this point only the most basic theses of the immaterialists have been articulated. Before the others he believes to be relevant to the discussion are included, the philosopher deals with the views of the materialists.

The philosopher has Theaetetus to play the part of a reasonable materialist, and leads him, in that capacity, to abandon the identification of being with body because he must admit that the virtues, which are not bodies, are beings. The argument is that since things that come to be present or absent in a thing are beings and the virtues come to be present or absent in the soul, it follows that the virtues are beings; but the virtues are not bodies. A reasonable materialist needs to realize, the philosopher believes, that being is what we have in view in calling both bodies and the virtues beings. What we have in view in calling both bodies and the virtues beings, he wants him to agree, is the form by participation in which a thing has to some degree the power to act upon something else or the power to be acted upon by something else even if only once.

Being, according to this definition of its nature, is that which possesses by itself the power to act upon something else or to be acted upon by something else. Let us call what has the power to act upon something else in this way a causal power. The qualifications included in this definition of being are important. By adding "even in the smallest degree," "the most insignificant thing," and "even if only once," Plato is cautioning the reader not to expect that the causal power he is talking about is the power to cause a recognizable change of place, quantity or quality in something else. In fact, he seems to want to have the philosopher claim, at 248A–E, that being itself has the power to be affected in this minimal way when it is being known by a soul. If we employ this definition to help us express a reasonable materialist's agreement that what we have in view in calling both bodies and the virtues beings is their causal powers, we may say that they agree that what we have in view, in calling both bodies and the virtues beings, is the form for being an agent that acts on an object or an object upon which an agent acts.

The argument used by the philosopher for this initial purpose begins by having the immaterialists assert, as two further theses to their theory, that being and what comes to be are other than one another because being is the same at all times and what comes to be is different at different times, and that the soul communes with what comes to be by means of sensation in the body and communes with being by means of her reasoning. I here render the philosopher's claim that "we" commune with what comes to be and being by different means as the claim that "the soul" does so because Plato believes that it is our souls that do so. In the *Theaetetus*, for instance, he makes it clear that our souls are the perceivers of things that continuously come to be by means of the sensations in their bodies and are the perceivers of being by means of reasonings that are present in them.

To commune with both what comes to be and being, however, souls must have the power to do so, and if they can commune with things that are so different in character, they must have two different powers, since the powers of the soul are different, as Plato tells us in the *Republic*, just in case the objects to which the exercise of these powers pertain are different. Each of these objects must also possess the power to have the soul commune with it.

The philosopher goes on to ask what the immaterialists could mean when they assert that the soul communes with that which comes to be and being. He wants to draw their attention to the fact that it will be the mutual actualization of the powers of the soul to commune with both that which comes to be and being and the powers of what comes to be and being to have souls commune with them. So the philosopher wants the immaterialists to accept the thesis that if souls commune with both that which comes to be and being, they commune with them by virtue of being agents that act on objects or objects that are acted upon by agents, and both that which comes to be and being are communed with by virtue of being such agents or objects. Hence, the philosopher would like to get the immaterialists to accept the thesis that the soul, what comes to be, and being are beings. If they should accept this thesis, they, like the materialists, would abandon their central thesis concerning the kind of thing being is, and realize that they have confused being with one of the things that is a being by virtue of partaking of being.

The immaterialists, however, prove to be less reasonable than their opponents, for they are represented as replying that although things that come to be can be agents or objects acted by agents, beings cannot. So the philosopher next attempts to get them to abandon this reply on the basis of their acceptance of another thesis they accept, which is that the soul has knowledge of being and being is known by the soul.

This thesis may in fact represent what the immaterialists meant to convey when they agreed the soul "communes" with being. Armed with this new information, the philosopher renews his effort to get them to agree that to be a being is to be an agent or an object acted upon by an agent. He is trying to get them to accept the view that if souls know a form, they know the form by virtue of being agents or objects acted by agents, and if the form is being known, it is being known by virtue of being an agent or an object acted on by an agent. If the philosopher can get them to accept this view, the way is open for them to accept the definition of being already provided.

The immaterialists, however, try to block this move by claiming that even though what comes to be can be an agent or an object acted upon an agent, being cannot be in motion when it is being known by the soul, since it is at rest. The implication of their statement, that being is at rest, is that it cannot be in motion, and so, that being is not in motion when it is being known by a soul. Instead of the immaterialists being made to consider the alternative thesis, that the soul, in knowing being, is in motion by virtue of knowing being, the philosopher suddenly begins to complain that their theory rules out the being of the soul, along with the being of motion, life and thought. The reason for this sudden complaint seems to be that the philosopher is being made to anticipate their answer to the question of whether or not the soul, which they believe, as Plato does, is self-moving, is a being. To be consistent, of course, they would have to deny that the soul is a being, and Plato has the philosopher complain about the anticipated answer to the question.

The philosopher does not at this point evaluate the immaterialists' answer to the first question, which concerned whether being is in motion when it is being known by the soul. Plato does in fact accept the view that being is in motion when it is being known by the soul, but he does not have the philosopher raise an objection to the denial that it is in motion when being known, since he does not wish to introduce a definition of motion to which the immaterialist may then object, and thereby steer the dialogue in a different direction. In fact, it is clear that he believes that the immaterialists' reason for rejecting the idea that being is in motion when it is being known by the soul is based on a confusion. The reason they give for being not being in motion when the soul is in the act of knowing it is that being is at rest. The assumption, that if being is at rest it cannot be in motion, involves a pair of errors, to one of which Plato will later call attention in the *Sophist*. The intended reader of the dialogue, he assumes, is aware of the errors involved in the immaterialists' reasoning at that point, and so he does not point them out, since if he should stop to identify these errors the discussion would turn in a different direction. What are these errors?

One error arises when it is said that a subject, which possesses a nature in relation to something else, has this nature, but without mentioning the fact that it possesses the nature in relation to something else. At 259C–D, where a summary is presented of the sorts of the errors that create the problems being discussed in the *Sophist*, Plato has the philosopher imply that when we say that a subject is both the same and other in some way, the sophist drops the qualification, "in some way" in order to make it appear as these are said of a subject without qualification. In its application to the immaterialists' denial that being is in motion because it is at rest, the error is to conclude, from the statement that being is at rest, the statement that it is not in motion, without specifying in what way being is at rest and in what way being is in motion. Although being cannot be both in motion and at rest in relation to the same thing, it can be both in motion and at rest in relation to different things.

The second error, the exposition of which can be used to make the first one more specific, is to make a claim about what can or cannot be in motion and at rest without defining the natures of motion and rest. Plato's modern translators and interpreters, perhaps along with the immaterialists, might be assuming that to be in motion is to change in place, quantity or quality. However, the definition of the nature of motion Plato himself would present, I believe, is that motion is the exercising of a causal power. The nature of rest, accordingly, is not that of not changing in place, quantity or quality, but to be the non-exercise of a causal power.

If we put these two definitions together with the fact that to be in motion or at rest is always to be so in relation to something else, to say that being is both in motion and at rest, for instance, is to say that its causal power is both being exercised, in relation to one thing, and not being exercised, in relation to something else. It is not necessarily true that the causal power that being is cannot both be and not be exercised, since its causal power can be exercised in relation to one thing and not be exercised in relation to another. Plato's view, in fact, seems to be that being is both in motion and at rest, but it is so in relation to different things.

In relation to a soul knowing it, it is in motion, since its power to be known is being exercised; but in relation to a soul not knowing it, it is at rest. Moreover, when a particular soul comes to know being, before it comes to know being, both being and this soul are at rest in relation to one another, and when this soul is knowing being, they are in motion in relation to one another. Again, being is in motion in relation to all of the forms of which it partakes and all of the things that partake of it, since its causal powers are being exercised in relation to both. Hence, when the immaterialists argue that if being is at rest it cannot be in motion, they fail both to specify in relation to what being is at rest and in relation to what being is in motion and also to define what motion and rest are.

At this point the philosopher himself is made to abandon the attempt to deal with the immaterialists' theory in the same way that he dealt with the materialists' theory. But the reason he abandons this attempt, as I have pointed out, is not that he thinks that the immaterialists are correct in denying that to be a being is to be an agent acting upon an object or an object acted upon by an agent. Since he need not get them to accept his account of being in order to make the point that to be a being is not to be a form, the philosopher simply argues that their reluctance to admit that being is in motion excludes the presence of motion, life, soul, and thought (*phronēsis*) in the perfect being (*to pantelōs on*). In other words, if they deny that what is in motion is a being because it is in motion, they must also deny that the perfect being possesses these other natures. How exactly the perfect being is in motion, however, is not explained. But to understand Plato's attempt to refute the immaterialists' thesis, we need to understand in what way Plato believes that it is. The key to understanding this we can find within the argument used to convince the immaterialists to abandon their claim that a being cannot be in motion.

The philosopher begins with the assumption that the immaterialists' theory implies that motion, life, soul and thought are not present in *to pantelōs on*. What exactly *to pantelōs on* refers to is not explained. That to which it refers, we may assume, is "that which is a being (*to on*) completely or perfectly (*pantelōs*)." On the assumption that I am right that for Plato to be a being is to possess causal power, that to which he is referring here is a being whose causal power is complete or perfect. Hence, I translate *to pantelōs on* as "the perfect being" in order to convey the idea that the being in question is what at 265C in the *Sophist* itself is called God and what in the *Timaeus* is called the divine craftsman. In fact, this being is the same as the "living creature" which, according to the *Timaeus*, is the model used by the divine craftsman to form an orderly sensible world from the disorderly motions that characterize the receptacle.

This living creature, Plato believes, is the divine craftsman himself, who is using his idea of himself as the model for his creation, which is also called a living creature. As a reference to this living creature, the claim that the perfect being is in motion, is alive, has soul and thought, and therefore, has mind, is intelligible. It is in motion, since it is continuously exercising its power to act upon the disorderly motions in the receptacle to produce an orderly sensible world. That it is alive, of course, follows from its description of being a living creature. The life it possesses, surely, is at least the life of its mind, which is the self-knowing it uses in order to make itself the model for the sensible living creature it creates. For this reason the philosopher says that it is alive because it possesses mind. The philosopher also says that it must possess soul if it possesses mind. Its soul, whose nature Plato identifies with self-motion, is the eternal exercise of the craftsman's power to create, as an image of himself, the sensible world. If it possesses soul, the philosopher says, it must possess motion. Here the idea is that the soul is the exercise of the power of the divine craftsman to create an image of the idea of himself in the receptacle. The implication of the explanation of *erōs* in the *Symposium* is that the soul, the exercise of this power, is a spontaneous response to the vision of the good.

Here I have presented only the barest sketch of Plato's doctrine that there is a perfect living creature of which the world revealed by sense is an imperfect copy. Useful information about this doctrine can be found in the second chapter of the first book of Aristotle's *De Anima* (404B16–28) and throughout the fifth ennead of Plotinus' *Enneads* (especially, tractates five, six, eight and nine). In the *Timeaus* itself Plato says little about the perfect living creature. Since his concern there is to explain the origin of the imperfect living creature, which is the sensible world, he concentrates upon the explanation of the soul and body of that creature.

When at 249B the philosopher concludes that beings cannot be without motion, since mind would not be present in anything or be concerned with anything, what Plato has in mind, surely, is that without the exercise of the power of the divine mind to conceive a world, the sensible world itself would not be the living creature it is, possessed of body and soul, and hence, possessed of mind, which is present in the soul of the sensible world. The conclusion the philosopher would have the immaterialists draw is that beings cannot be only at rest.

Upon drawing this conclusion, the philosopher considers the claim that all things are coming to be and are in motion. He says that this claim also implies that there is no mind present in anything or concerned with anything. The reason he gives for this implication is that if all things were without rest, things would never come to be the same in number, quality, or relation, and if things were never to come to be the same in number, quality, or relation, mind could not be a being or come to be anywhere.

He does not explain why things would not come to be the same in number, quality or relation if all were without rest. The reason seems to be that if all things were without rest, the constant and pervasive exercise of the causal powers of all beings would make it impossible for anything to stay the same in any respect for any length of time. It is not clear what the philosopher means when he says that if things were never to come to be the same in number, quality or relation, mind could not be a being or come to be anywhere. Part of what it means, perhaps, is that if sensible objects never came to be the same in number, quality or relation, the power to cause them to be the same in number, quality or relation would never be exercised, which would imply that there is no mind, which is the being that possess such a causal power, and so, no mind that could come to be present in the soul of the sensible world.

In his next statement, the philosopher says that they should reject all claims that imply that knowledge, thought and mind are not beings. Although he had not yet explicitly argued that knowledge and thought would not be beings if all beings were at rest or all beings were in motion, he thinks he is entitled to draw this conclusion because he has already argued that mind would not be a being unless not all beings are at rest and not all beings are in motion. If there is no mind, there is no knowledge or thought. The conclusion drawn at 249C–D is that all beings are at rest and are in motion. The sense in which Plato thinks that this is true is that all being are at rest and in motion in relation to different things. However, the qualification, "in relation to different things," is not included in the philosopher's statement of the conclusion.

The objection to being (249D–250E)

At 249D–250E, after his expressing satisfaction with the account of being presented earlier, that to be a being is to be an agent or an object acted upon by an agent, the philosopher suddenly announces that they once again face an objection. This time the objection concerns how being itself can be. To introduce the objection the philosopher raises the same question about his own conclusion that he posed about the enumeration of the primary beings given by the pluralists. He introduces the objection so that he can go on to expose a confusion that might be used to deny that being is one of the self-natured beings that cause other things to possess their attributes.

The argument of the objection, which I will call the objection to being, begins with the assertion that being is other than motion and rest. The philosopher first says that since motion and rest are contraries and motion and rest are beings, being is other than motion and rest, since if it were the same as one or the other of these contraries, the other would not be a being, and if it were the same as both, being would possess contrary natures. But if being is other than motion and rest, the philosopher concludes, then "being, according to its own nature, is neither in motion nor at rest" (*kata tēn hautou physin ara to on oute kesteken oute kineitai*). This statement simply means that the nature of being is not to be in motion or at rest. According to my interpretation of what the definition is of these forms, the meaning is that to possess causal powers is not the same as either to exercise them or not to exercise them.

But now the philosopher says that if being, according to its own nature, is neither in motion nor at rest, being is neither in motion nor at rest. Hence, it seems to follow that being cannot be an object of discourse or thought, since whatever can be made an object of discourse or thought must be either in motion or at rest. But being is, of course, other than motion and rest. So at 250D–E the conclusion is drawn that being has turned out to be as perplexing as non-being.

Why is the objection to being introduced at this point in the philosopher's attempt to deal with Parmenides' denial of the being of non-being? It is introduced, first of all, in order to present us with yet another example of a sophistic argument in which a false conclusion appears to follow from what appear to be true premises. Plato believes that the objection to being suffers from two different faults. He thinks that it is faulty because it involves a fallacious move of the sort the sophists often make in their arguments and because some sophists believe that the move, in this particular argument, can be justified on the basis of a view about naming.

The fallacious move of the sort the sophists often make in their arguments is to assert a true premise in which a subject is qualified in some way, and then later in the argument to drop the qualification, making the premise false, and so making it appear, to someone unskilled in argument, that he is committed to an absurd conclusion that is drawn from the premises to which he has agreed. In the objection to being, the qualification dropped is "according to its own nature." Although the premise whose subject is qualified in this way is true, the premise in which the qualification is dropped is false. Theaetetus, however, is unaware of the change. Theaetetus' agreement to a true premise is made to be an agreement to a false premise.

In addition, according to Plato, there are sophists who would claim that the dropping of this qualification in the argument is justified. They would claim that the dropping of this qualification is justified on the basis of the argument that a single-natured thing like a form cannot be called by a name other than the name it receives according to its own nature, since the only basis upon which it can be named is the single nature it possesses by itself. Since this claim, Plato believes, is false, it cannot be used to justify the dropping of the qualification, "according to its own nature," from the premise that "being, according to its own nature, is neither in motion nor at rest."

The claim that Plato thinks some sophists would make to justify the dropping of this qualification has been attributed to the sophist, Antisthenes. This sophist apparently claimed that one thing cannot be many, meaning by this that a single-natured thing cannot be many things, and so, that it can be called only by its own name, since every name signifies just one nature a thing possesses. Plato himself believes that his single-natured forms are assigned their names on the basis of the natures they alone independently possess. But he also thinks that they can be called by the names of other forms of which they partake. Hence, Plato's reply to the problem of being is to argue that even though each form receives a name on the basis of the nature it alone possesses by itself, it also receives the names of the forms of which it partakes.

At 250E–251A, the philosopher concludes, that since being would seem to be as problematic as the objection to non-being made out non-being to be, there is hope that whatever light he can shed on the one may help to make clear the other and in the process answer the objection to classifying a sophist as a dealer in falsehood and images. Before Plato presents his joint illumination of being and non-being, however, he has the philosopher argue, on the assumption that every form possesses a distinct nature of its own, that each is called by the name of the forms of which it partakes, and then, that being, motion and rest are other than one another because they partake of the other in relation to one another, not by their own natures. The first argument reveals the false view that underlies the objection to being, and the second prepares the basis for the joint illumination of being and non-being. The philosopher is then made to state his conclusions and to issue warnings about the tricks of a sophist such as those he employed in explaining the difficulties that arise for accounts of images and falsehoods and in presenting the objection to being.

At 251A–254B, the philosopher argues that one thing can be called by many names because when one form combines with many others it receives their names in addition to its own, but some forms cannot be called by the names of forms that possess natures contrary to their own. He adds that not only the sophists, but also all parties to the disputes concerning the number of beings there are and the nature of being must admit that some forms can combine with others if they are to state their own views, since only if one forms can combine with one another can the sophists and the others state their views. Finally, he briefly explains the sort of knowledge of the forms he is about to use in presenting his response to the objection to being.

At 254B–255E, the philosopher presents an argument for a premise he needs for the joint illumination of being and non-being. He introduces five forms of which all other forms partake: being, motion, rest, the same in relation to itself or to something else, and the other in relation to something else. Each of these forms other than the other in relation to something else, he argues, is other than the others, since it partakes of the other in relation to the others rather than because of its own nature. Having shown that being, motion, rest and the same in relation to itself or to something else partake of the other in relation to one another, Plato has the philosopher refer to motion partaking of the other in relation to something else, X, as motion partaking of "a non-X."

Hence, the philosopher now can say that motion partaking of the other in relation to being is motion partaking of "a non-being." In fact, any form partaking of the other in relation to being the philosopher can now call "a non-being." Plato has now created the terminology he needs in order to illuminate both being and non-being. So now, at 255E-257A, he has the philosopher argue that being and everything that partakes of being is a non-being and that non-being, defined as that which by its own nature is other with respect to a being, is a being.

The reply to the objection to being (251A–254B)

The objection to being was based on the view that being cannot be in motion or at rest because it is not in motion or at rest according to its own nature. Plato has the philosopher reply to this objection by showing that in spite of being not being in motion or rest according to its own nature, it can be in motion or at rest, since it can be called not only by the name of its own nature, but also by the names of the forms of which it partakes. He shows this simply by arguing that one thing can be called by many names.

The view against Plato has the philosopher argue has been attributed to the sophist, Antisthenes. This sophist is thought to have argued that something cannot be called by any name other than the name of its own nature, since a name is assigned to something only on the basis of the nature it possesses by itself.[29] This is the basis upon which the philosopher is made to say that those who accept the view that one thing cannot be many "forbid us to call a man good, but to allow us only to call the good good and a man man."

The premise in the objection to being that enables the philosopher, playing the role of a sophist, to draw the conclusion, that being is unnamable and unthinkable, is that the names of motion and rest cannot be applied to being because being, according to its own nature, is neither in motion nor at rest. Plato has the philosopher assert this premise on the basis of the view that only the name applied to being according to its own nature can be applied to it. So the reply to the objection is to show that this view is false. It is shown, in particular, that a form can be called not only by the name it receives because of its own nature, but also by the names of the forms of which it partakes.

At 251A–D the philosopher says that there are those who explicitly argue that something cannot be both one and many and on this basis conclude that it is a mistake to call one thing by many names. The view that something cannot be both one and many is based on the view that none of the most elemental things can possess more than one nature on the basis of which it is named.

The philosopher's argument against this view has two parts. The first part of the argument is that if it is not granted that something can be both one and many by reason of one form combining with many others, the views of the pluralists, the monists, the materialists, the immaterialists and the sophists who deny that one thing can be called by many names could not even be stated. Those who claim that all beings are in motion without being at rest must grant that motion combines with being and those who claim that all beings are at rest without must grant that rest combines with being. Furthermore, a sophist who denies that one thing can be called by many names will have refuted himself by stating his own view, which requires one thing to be called by the name of another. Therefore, if they wish to make statements at all, they must admit that some forms combine with others. The second part of the argument is presented by Theaetetus, who claims that all must grant that things like motion and rest cannot combine with one another because of their contrariety. The two parts of the argument, Plato believes, establish the need for a real distinction between things that can combine with one another and things that cannot.

At 252E–254B, Plato has the philosopher give a brief account of the type of knowledge of the combinatory powers of forms required to continue the investigation and claim that it is the true philosopher or dialectician rather than the sophist who possesses this knowledge. It has just been argued, of course, that some forms can combine and others cannot. The philosopher now says that it is the true philosopher or dialectician who has knowledge of which forms can combine and which cannot. He likens the powers of forms to accept and reject combination to the powers of letters of the alphabet to accept and reject combination. Just as the grammarian knows, by knowing the causal powers of the letters, which letters can combine and which cannot, so the dialectician knows, by knowing the causal powers of the forms, which forms can combine and which cannot.

The philosopher also says at 253A that the dialectician knows which forms are like vowels, which are letters that bind other letters together that could not otherwise be combined. Because each of these vowel-like forms combines with all other forms, including the other vowel-like forms, the others are able to combine with one another. Although the philosopher does not explicitly say which forms are the vowel-like forms, his subsequent discussion makes it clear that they are being, motion, rest, the same in relation to itself or to something else and the other in relation to something else.

Being, the philosopher has already suggested, may be defined as the form that causes all other forms to possess causal powers by combining with it. Being, which possesses causal power by its own nature, causes all forms with which it combines to possess causal power. Causal power, Plato believes, is the power to be acted upon by something or to act upon something. Though Plato does not have the philosopher define them, the definitions of motion, rest, the same and the other can easily be reconstructed, as I have above, on the basis of this definition of being.

Motion, I have suggested, is that which by its own nature is the exercise of a causal power. What partakes of motion is exercising a causal power it possesses by virtue of partaking of being. What exercises a causal power, moreover, exercises it in relation to something because its causal power is its power to be acted upon by something or to act upon something. Plato believes that what partakes of motion may partake of motion in relation to itself or in relation to something else. The soul partakes of motion in relation to itself, while the body partakes of motion in relation to another body and ultimately in relation to the soul, which in the *Phaedrus* and the *Laws* is said to be the first cause of all motion of bodies. The fact that a thing can partake of motion by itself or in relation to something else does not change the nature of motion, which by its own nature is the exercise of an active or passive causal power in relation to something.

Rest may be defined as that which by its own nature is the non-exercise of causal power. What partakes of rest is what is not exercising a causal power in relation to something. Although being, for instance, is at rest in relation to a soul that is not at a given time knowing it, it may be in motion in relation to different soul that is knowing it at the same time. So being can be both at rest and in motion in relation to different things.

The same may be defined as that which by its own nature is the same as itself or the same as something else. For a thing by itself to partake of the same is for it to be the same as itself, but for it to partake of the same in relation to another thing is for it to be the same as the other thing. If one form combines with another, of course, it must be the same as itself. No form partakes of the same in relation to another form, it seems, since no two forms possess the very same nature. When one form is called by different names, it is still the same in relation to itself, though we may say, because of the two different names assigned to the same thing, that one thing is the same as another.

Finally, the other is that which by its own nature is other in relation to something else. That which partakes of the other in relation to something else is said to be other than it. Since no form can partake of another form unless it is other than the form of which it partakes, no form can partake of itself. Since being is other than motion and rest by virtue of partaking of the other in relation to both, rather than by its own nature, being can partake of both motion and rest at different times, if in relation to the same thing, or at the same time, if in relation to different things.

At 253D the dialectician is said to be the one who knows how forms can and cannot combine, since he is able to discern a form of which all other forms partake ("everywhere extended through many"), the many forms that partake of it ("embraced from without by one"), forms that combine with other forms ("connected in a unity though many"), and forms that do not combine because they are contraries ("entirely marked off apart").[30]

The otherness of the other greatest kinds (254B–255E)

At 254B–C, the philosopher decides to examine the causal powers of being, motion and rest to accept and reject combination in order to show that each is other than the others because it partakes of the other in relation to the others rather than because of its own nature. (Although motion and rest are other than one another because of their own natures, they are, nonetheless, also other than one another because they partake of the other in relation to one another.) If two forms combine, he assumes, they possess the causal power to combine, and if they do not, they do not possess the causal power to combine. The purpose of his examination of the causal powers of being, motion and rest to combine is to show that each combines with the other in relation to the others. In this way, he shows that the other in relation to another is a distinct form.

In the process of examining the causal powers of being, motion and rest to accept and reject combination, the philosopher also refers both to their otherness in relation to one another and to their sameness in relation to themselves. The examination of the causal powers not only of being, motion and rest, but also the same and the other to combine, Plato believes, will enable the philosopher to provide a joint illumination of being and non-being. The examination takes the form of an argument whose four premises are themselves backed by arguments, most of which pose difficult problems of interpretation. So it will be convenient to set out the overarching argument before giving a detailed analysis of the arguments for each of the premises. The argument may be set out as follows:

(1) Being, motion and rest are other than one another and the same as themselves.
(2) The same and the other are other than motion and rest.
(3) The same is other than being.
(4) The other is other than being.

Therefore,

(5) Being, motion, rest and the same are other than one another because they partake of the other, not because of their own natures.

It will be noticed that I have recast the philosopher's own statement of the conclusion of this argument into a form that makes it clear that, when at 255E he says that the other "pervades all," he means all of the others.

The argument for premise (1), presented at 254D–E, is that being, motion, and rest must be three in number, since motion and rest, as contraries, cannot combine and being can combine with both, and since they are three in number, each is the same as itself and other than the others. By saying that each is the same as itself and other than the others because they are three in number he shows that by the same as itself he means the same in number as itself and by other than the others he means other in number than one another The conclusion of the argument follows from these premises if we assume (i) that a form that cannot combine with another form must be other than it, (ii) that a form that combines with another form must be the same as itself, and (iii) that a form that combines with both of a pair of contrary forms must be other than each one individually, since if it were the same as either one, which is contrary to the other, contrary forms could combine, which is impossible.

The argument for premise (2) is presented at 254E–255B. The philosopher argues that the same and the other are other than motion and rest, since motion and rest, as contraries, cannot combine, but both the same and the other can combine with both, which would not be possible if the same or the other was one or the other. The same assumptions are again operative in this argument as in the last, and in this case, in fact, he makes (iii) explicit.

If when the philosopher says that something partakes of the same, he means that something partake of the same either in relation to itself or in relation to something else, he is absolved of an error he has been thought to have committed in the argument for premise (3). In the argument for premise (3), which occurs at 255B–C, it is said that the same is other than being, since if it were not, to say that motion and rest are beings would mean that they are the same, which is impossible. It has been claimed that the philosopher has equivocated on "the same," since after arguing that motion and rest are *the same as themselves* because they partake of the same, the philosopher then argues that if the same were the same as being, to say that motion and rest are beings is to say that they are *the same as one another*, which is impossible. Hence, it has been claimed, Plato's argument is invalid.

Plato's argument is not invalid, since in his view, when each of two things separately partakes of the same, each is the same as itself, but when two things partake of the same in relation to one another, they are the same as one another. The argument for premise (3) is that if "the same" were just another name for that of which "being" is a name, then since attributing sameness to two things means that they are the same as one another, saying that motion and rest are beings is to say that motion and rest are the same as one another.

The argument for premise (4), presented at 255C–E, is that the other must be other than being, since some beings are spoken of by themselves (*legesthai auta kath' hauta*), while other beings are always spoken of in relation to other things (*aei legesthai pros alla*), but what is other is always spoken of in relation to something else. The difference is that what partakes of being may partake of it either by itself or in relation to something else, but what partakes of the other always partakes of it in relation to something else.

The philosopher is not made to argue here that there are two forms of being, one non-relational and the other relational. Instead, he is made to call attention to a difference between how being and otherness are attributed to things. These different ways of attributing being and otherness to things are due to the fact that being is not by its own nature a relational form, while the other is. An example of a relational attribution of being to something is to say that sitting is a being in relation to Theaetetus if Theaetetus is sitting, while a non-relational attribution of being to something is to say that the Theaetetus who is sitting is a being. Being is attributed to sitting in relation to Theaetetus and to Theaetetus himself apart from a relation he has to something else.[31] Plato, therefore, does not believe, as Aristotle, does, that "being" has different senses. His view is that there are two ways in which something can partake of being, not that there are two senses of "being."

Since Plato does not believe that any form partakes of itself, the next premise of the argument for (4) is not that the other is other than being because it partakes of itself in relation to being. In the *Phaedo*, Socrates is made to say that what is the beautiful, other than the beautiful itself, is beautiful because it partakes of the beautiful. The beautiful, it is assumed, is by its own nature beautiful, and anything else that is beautiful is so because it partakes of the beautiful. Similarly, the other is other than being by its own nature, since its nature is to be the other in relation to anything else to which it is set in contrast.

The proof that being is a non-being (255E–257A)

At 250E–251A, the philosopher said that he would try to present a joint illumination of being and non-being. The first phase of the illumination is to argue that being is a non-being. At 255E8–256A2, the philosopher begins this argument by claiming that motion is a non-rest (*kinēsis ou stasis estin*) because it is completely other than rest, and that it is a being (*kinēsis estin*) because it partakes of being. Motion here is said to be completely other than rest for emphasis, since motion and rest are contraries. Nonetheless, in this argument, since the philosopher says that motion is a non-rest, he is saying that motion is a non-rest because it partakes of the other in relation to rest.

The fact that Plato places the negation sign, *ou*, before *stasis* rather than before *estin,* in the claim, *kinēsis ou stasis estin*, shows that he construes *ou stasis* as a name that signifies the other in relation to what is at rest by its own nature. This premise of the argument, however, is usually mistranslated as "Motion is not rest," which makes it into a statement of negative identity. The use of the negation sign before *stasis* in the sentence shows that *ou stasis* is that of which *kinēsis* partakes. Of course, Plato does not deny that the negation sign may also be used to negate a sentence in which *stasis* is predicated of *kinēsis*, since he does not deny that one form can fail to partake of another. He most certainly knows that *kinēsis stasis ouk estin*, in ordinary Greek, means "Motion is not rest." But instead of using this sentence, he chooses the sentence *kinēsis ou stasis estin*, which means that motion partakes of non-rest.

Plato's use of *ou stasis* is rendered here by the barbarism, "a non-rest." It is translated "a non-rest" rather than "non-rest," since to translate the sentence in which it occurs as "Motion is non-rest," transforms Plato's use of the "is" of participation into the use of the "is" of identity. What the sentence means, Plato believes, is that motion partakes of the other in relation to rest," which is his analysis of the sentence, "Motion is a non-rest."

The awkwardness of "a non-rest" is matched by the awkwardness of *ou stasis* in Greek. It may have been because of this awkwardness, in addition to not understanding what Plato meant by this sentence, that other translators and commentators adopted the alternative of treating *ou* as a sign of the negation of the sentence as a whole. This awkwardness of translation is the price to be paid for a clear understanding of what the problem is Plato is trying to solve and how he goes about solving the problem in the argument of which "Motion is a non-rest" is a premise. At this point in the *Sophist* he is assigning a special meaning to negated terms rather than clarifying the meaning of negated sentences or negated participation in a form.

The philosopher continues at 256A3–9 by arguing that it is possible to say that motion is the same, since it partakes of the same, and that it is a non-the same (*ou tauton estin*), since it partakes of the other in relation to the same. (Once again, the awkwardness of the English translation matches that of the Greek.) He gives the following explanation, in whose translation I have retained the Greek for "the same" and "a non-the same" to make it clear that he consistently places the negative sign in one of its forms before *tauton* rather than before the verb of his sentences.

> Then we must agree without dissent that indeed motion is both *tauton* and *ou tauton*. For when we say this, we do not use *tauton* and *ou tauton* in the same way. For we say that it is *tauton* because it partakes of *tauton* in relation to itself, and that it is *mē tauton* because of its communion with the other, because of which, since it is separate from *tauton*, it does not become that but other, with the consequence that it is also correct to say that it is *ou tauton*. (256A10–256B4)

What does it mean to use *tauton* and *ou tauton* in the same way? But because they are being used in the same way, Plato implies, the statement in question would be equivalent to the claim that motion is both the same in relation to itself and not the same in relation to itself, which is impossible.

At 256B the philosopher calls attention to the distinction between contraries, such as motion and rest, and non-contraries, such as the same and non-the same, by saying that it would not be absurd to assert that motion is at rest if it could partake of rest. His point is that if motion and rest were not contraries, but instead merely other than one another, motion could partake of rest. When at 256B–C the philosopher recalls the proof that some forms combine, and others do not, he is simply reminding Theaetetus that forms that are not contraries, such as the same and the non-the same, can combine.

The philosopher's survey is quickly completed by claiming that we can say that motion is (i) an other (*heteron*, 256C5), since it partakes of the other in relation to the same and to rest, (ii) a non-other (*ouch heteron*, 256C8), since it partakes of the other than the other, (iii) both a non-being and a being (*ouk on kai on,* 256D8–9), since it partakes of the other in relation to being and partakes of being. Because motion is other in relation to being, it is said to be a non-being. Since in these sentences the "is" of participation is employed, none is a statement of identity.

The first conclusion the philosopher draws from these premises I have translated as follows:

> PHIL. Therefore, non-being must be a being in relation both to motion and to all the kinds [other than being]. For in relation to all of the [other] kinds, the nature of the other renders each a non-being (*ouk on*) by making it other than a being, and so, in the same way, we may correctly say of all of them [other than being] that they are non-beings (*ouk onta*),

> and again, that they both are and are beings (*einai te kai onta*) because they partake of being.
> THT. That seems to be true.
> PHIL. In relation to each of the forms [other than being], therefore, being is many in number and non-being is unlimited in number (256D11–E3)

To say that a non-being is a being in relation to motion means that motion is a non-being that is a being. Motion is a non-being that is a being in the sense that it partakes of the other in relation to being and also partakes of being. All forms other than being are said to be non-beings in the sense that they are other than being. All forms other than being are beings because they partake of being. The philosopher is saying that not only of motion, but all forms other than being, both non-being and being are predicated.

At 256E the philosopher then draws a second conclusion. It is the conclusion that in relation to each of the forms other than being, being is many in number and non-being is countless in number.[32] To say that being is many in number in relation to each of the forms other than being means that each form is as many beings as there are beings, other than being itself, of which it partakes. This conclusion seems to be a generalization drawn from the fact that it has been shown that motion partakes of non-rest, the same, the non-the same, the other, and the non-other, all of which are beings other than being itself. Since there is only a limited number of beings of which not only motion, but of which every other form other than being, partakes, it is said that being is many in number in relation to each of the forms other than being. Since these are beings and motion partakes of them, being is predicated of motion as many times as there are beings of which it partakes.

To say that non-being is countless in number in relation to each of the forms other than being means that each form is countless non-beings because it is other in relation to the countless things that are other than being. This conclusion is a generalization drawn from the fact that it has been shown that motion partakes of the other in relation to rest, the same, and the other, each of which is other than being. Just as it is a non-being in relation to these forms, so it is a non-being in relation to the countless forms other than being.

After having argued that all forms other than being itself are non-beings, at 257A the philosopher shows that since being itself is other in relation to all of the forms that partake of it, being too is a non-being, since all of the form that partake of it are beings. In drawing this conclusion he fulfills his intention to prove that being is a non-being. He has in fact argued that every being, including being itself, is a non-being.

The proof that non-being is a being (257B–258C)

At 257B–C, the philosopher argues the non-being is as much a being as being is. Since he believes that he has shown that every form, including being itself, is countlessly many non-beings, he infers that when we speak of a non-being, we are not speaking of that which is contrary to a being but only of what is other than a being. The assumption of the objection to the being of a non-being, Plato believes, has now been shown to be false. He has the philosopher argue, by analogy, that non-being is not the contrary of being.

The philosopher claims that to say that something is non-large does not imply that "non-large" signifies the natures of either the small or the medium-sized, which are contrary to the nature of the large. The point is that "non-" in "non-large," it does not signify the possession of a nature contrary to the natures of the small or the medium-sized. We are to infer that something is a non-being does not imply that "non-" in "non-being" signifies a nature contrary to the nature of being. In general, he concludes, at 257B–C, we must not accept the view that "non-" in "non-X" signifies contrariety to, rather than otherness than, the nature signified when "X" is applied to something..

At 257C–258C, the philosopher fulfills his promise to prove that there is a sense in which non-being is itself a being and shows, in the process, how his conclusion about the signification of "non" applies to non-being itself. Even though he has argued that every form is both a being and a non-being and that when we speak of a non-being we are not speaking of what is contrary to a being, he has not yet proved that non-being itself is a being, which he said he would establish at 241D6–7. A proof for this thesis, he thinks, requires that he show that non-being is a form. Since non-being is a form if it has a nature of its own, he shows that non-being has a nature of its own.

When at 237B–E the philosopher first conducted a search for something to which "non-being" is applied, his search was blocked by the assumption that non-being is contrary to being. Now that he has shown that non-being is not contrary to being and that all forms are both beings and non-beings, he wants to explain how non-being possesses a nature of its own so that he can prove that it too is a form that possesses being. He begins the explanation at 257C–D. He claims that the nature of the other is like knowledge, which is divided, without loss of its unity, into parts, each of which is distinguished from the others by a special name. He believes that just as the part of knowledge that is set in contrast to numbers is called knowledge of numbers, in the same way, for instance, the part of the nature of the other set in contrast to the nature of the beautiful is called the non-beautiful.

The non-beautiful, he says, is a contrast (*antithesis*, 257E6) between a part of the nature of the other and the nature of the beautiful (*tēs tou kalou physeōs*, 257D11). Since we are told at 255D1 that the other is always the other "in relation to something else" (*pros heteron*), the non-beautiful is said to be the other than something else that is a beautiful thing. In other words, the non-beautiful is the other than something that is beautiful. That which is other than a beautiful thing may or may not itself be beautiful, since the otherness in question is simply numerical difference. The non-beautiful, therefore, is not the other than *the form*, the beautiful; it is the other than something that is beautiful, where this something may or may not be the beautiful itself.

It is essential to the philosopher's argument, therefore, that his account of the non-beautiful be understood so that the same thing can partake of both the beautiful and the non-beautiful, just as the same thing can partake of both being and non-being. In 255E–256E, Plato took "a non-rest," "a non-the same," "a non-other," and "a non-being" to refer to what partakes of the other than that which is at rest, than that which is the same with respect to something, than that which is other with respect to something else, and than that which is a being. It just so happened that in these cases that to which the other was set in contrast were the forms of rest, the same, the other and being. This is also true of what is non-beautiful. The part of the nature of the other that is a contrast to the nature of the beautiful is an otherness than something that is beautiful, just as, for instance, the part of the nature of the other than is a contrast to the nature of rest is an otherness than something that is at rest.

When the philosopher says that part of the nature of the other is "set in contrast" to the nature of the beautiful, he means to be referring to the act of someone contrasting a subject to something that is beautiful. So even the beautiful itself may be contrasted by someone to the things that are beautiful because they partake of the beautiful. In performing this act, he is saying that the beautiful partakes of the non-beautiful, since the beautiful itself is other than the other things that are beautiful. Just so, being itself may be contrasted by someone to the things that are beings because they partake of being. In performing this act, he is saying that being partakes of non-being because being is other than other beings. Moreover, just as there are many beautiful things by reason of each being non-beautiful in relation to the others, so there are many beings by reason of each being a non-being in relation to the others.[33]

The nature of the non-beautiful is a being, the philosopher continues at 257E, because it is a contrast of a certain sort someone can make. At 258A he says that just as the nature of the non-beautiful is a being that is a contrast to something that is beautiful, and so is as much a being as is the being to which it is contrasted, so every part of the nature of the other, for example, the non-tall, the non-just, and so forth, is as much a being as the being to which it is contrasted. Since the nature of the other has been shown to be a being, the philosopher adds, the parts of its nature must also be beings.

Plato now has the philosopher (i) identify non-being as one part of the nature of the other, (ii) conclude that it itself is a being that is not contrary to any being to which it is set in contrast, and (iii) claim that this non-being is the very one whose being he needed to establish in order to reply to the objection to the classification of a sophist as a dealer in false images and falsehoods.

> PHIL. Then it seems that the contrast in which a part of the nature of the other and the nature of being are set against one another is, if we may speak in this way, a being no less than is being itself [to whose nature the part of the nature of the other is set in contrast], since the contrast does not signify what is contrary to being, but only what is other in relation to it.
> THEA. That is very clear.
> PHIL. Then what shall we call it?
> THEA. It is evident that it is the very non-being for which we were searching because of the sophist. (258A11–B7)

So non-being, the philosopher concludes, is a being. It is that part of the nature of the other that is a contrast to the nature of being. This means that non-being is the form by participation in which something is other than something else that is a being. This form is a substance (*ousia*), the philosopher says, since it has a nature of its own, just as being does. Hence, he can say that non-being is a being, and so, that it can be named and made an object of thought.

The philosopher concludes that his investigation of the powers of being, motion, and rest to accept and reject combination has shown, as he hoped it would at 254C–D, that non-being is a being precisely because it itself really is a non-being, i.e. that it is by its own nature a non-being. Since the beautiful really is beautiful and the non-beautiful really is non-beautiful, they are kinds or forms that are beings. In the same way, he says, non-being is one form (*eidos hen*, 258C3) among the many, all of which are beings. He has proved, therefore, that non-being is a being.

Summary of argument and call to abandon sophistry

(258C-260D)

At 258C6–259D8, the philosopher summarizes this account of non-being. He points out that he has not only established that non-being is not contrary to being, but also proved that non-being is that part of the nature of the other that is a contrast to each thing as a being. He challenges others to find, without reliance upon sophistic counter-arguments, what is wrong with the argument that led to his account, and if they cannot find good counter-arguments, to accept his argument. He has shown not only that forms can combine with one another, but also that being and the other can combine with one another and with all other forms, with the result that both they themselves and all the others are, in relation to many things, beings and non-beings.

The sophistic counter-arguments to which the philosopher refers are those "dragging words sometimes to one thing and at other times to another." Here he is referring to the practice of "always bringing contraries into discussions" without specifying "in each case the way in which, and in relation to what" these contraries are mentioned. Examples of this practice are their claims that "the same is other, that the other is the same, that the large is small, or that the like is unlike." These statements, the philosopher implies, are not contrary to themselves, since in them it is not mentioned in which way, or in relation to what, these contraries are related, and when this information is supplied, the illusion of their being statements that are contrary to themselves is dispelled. His point is that the same can be said to be other in relation to other things, that the other can be said to be the same in relation to itself, that the large in relation to a man can be said to be small in relation to a building, and the like in relation to one attribute can be said to be unlike in relation to another.

The proof that there are falsehoods and images (260D–264D)

The philosopher now thinks that he has shown that he can explain what falsehoods are without being forced to assume that contraries can combine. However, even if he can explain what falsehoods are, there may in fact not be any falsehoods. So a sophist may protest that unless it is proved that there are falsehoods, the classification of the sophist as a dealer in falsehoods may still be challenged. It is for this reason that the philosopher argues, at 260D–264B, that there are falsehoods.

The philosopher begins at 260D–261C by pointing out the need for this argument and the general form it should take. The need for the argument, of course, is to prevent a sophist from aborting his classification as a dealer in falsehood. The argument for the existence of false discourse, he says, has been made easier by his proof that there is discourse. He proved that there is discourse when he argued that one thing can be called by many names. If it can be proved that there is false discourse, Plato believes, it can easily be proved that there are false beliefs and false perceptual judgments, and if these exist, that there are false images, since there must be false images of the truth if there are falsehoods.

The proof that there are falsehoods, it is said at 260B, requires that it be proved that non-being combines with belief (*doxa*) and discourse (*logos*). What it means for non-being to combine with belief and discourse is not clear. If the arguments to follow are an indication of its meaning, it means that what is believed and said to be, in relation to a subject, combines with non-being in relation to the subject or that what is believed or said to be a non-being in relation to a subject combines with being in relation to the subject. To proof this, the philosopher says, he will need to explain what belief and discourse are. And since he wanted to show that appearing to be can combine with non-being, he adds that he will need to explain what perceptual judgment is. Appearing to be combines with non-being in the sense that what appears to be a being is other than the being it appears to be.

At 261C–262E the philosopher provides the explanation of the nature of discourse. The elements of discourse, he says, are words or names (*onomata*, 261D4). Like the forms, some can combine and others cannot. In the case of words, what is produced is discourse rather than another name, or even a list of names, which cannot, as discourse can, accomplish something (*ti perainei*, 262D4), namely, show (*deloi*, 262D2) us something about beings in the present, past, or future rather than merely mark them off from one another in the way names do. To produce discourse of the most elementary kind, he says, one must combine a name, which is used to signify what performs an action, with a verb, which is used to signify the action performed.

At 262E3–263B4, "Theaetetus sits" and "Theaetetus flies" are chosen as examples of elementary true and false discourse. The first of these sentences shows about Theaetetus that sitting is a being in relation to him at the time the sentence is being uttered, and the second shows about Theaetetus that flying is a being in relation to him at the time the sentence is being uttered. If there is no Theaetetus, the philosopher says, neither of the above two utterances are discourse, since the being of discourse requires that there be a being about which it shows something.

If "Theaetetus sits" and "Theaetetus flies" are discourse, he then claims, they must be of a certain kind (*poion tina,* 262E8), namely, discourse that is true or false. His explication of the kinds of these two examples of discourse will be the final part of his account of the nature of discourse, and is meant to provide us, in effect, with a definition of the nature of discourse comparable to that which he seeks for the nature of a sophist. From his own point of view, therefore, by showing that these pieces of discourse are of the kinds, true and false, he will "demonstrate" that discourse, by its very nature, is utterance that is true or false. By discourse, in this case, he means elementary statements.

Plato says that "Theaetetus sits" is true because it is of the sort that says that things that are beings in relation to Theaetetus are beings in relation to him (263B4–5). In other words, it says that sitting is a being in relation to him, and since this is a being in relation to him, the statement is true. By contrast, he says, "Theaetetus flies" is false because it is of the sort that says that things other than beings in relation to Theaetetus are beings in relation to him (263B7). In other words, this statement says that flying, which is a being other than a being in relation to Theaetetus, is a being in relation to him, and so is false. The philosopher then shows that non-being combines with being in the account of falsehood in statements by substituting *ta mē onta* for *heteron tōn ontōn* in this characterization. This shows that when he spoke of beings other than beings in relation to Theaetetus, he was speaking of non-beings in relation to Theaetetus (263B9). So "Theaetetus flies" is false because it says that flying, which is a non-being in relation to Theaetetus, is a being in relation to him. In securing this result Plato has fulfilled his intention to show that non-being combines with what is said to be a being, and hence his intention to prove that there is falsehood in discourse.

To underscore the fact that this reference to non-beings in his conclusion has already been shown to be unproblematic, at 263B11 the philosopher substitutes *ontōn hetera* for *to mē onta*, and justifies the substitution by pointing out that he has already proved that in relation to each thing there are many beings and many non-beings (*polla men gar ephamen onta peri hekaston einai pou, polla de ouk onta*, 263B11–12). He is referring here back to 256E5–6 (and indirectly to 259D5–6), where he concluded that in relation to each of the forms, being is many in number and non-being is unlimited in number. This statement we have already seen to be equivalent to the statement that each of the forms is both many beings and countless non-beings. Plato here has the claim be made about "each thing" rather than about "each of the forms," since he thinks that if each of the forms is many beings and countless non-beings, each thing that partakes of a form is also many beings and countless non-beings. He is pointing out now that his reference to non-beings in his account of false discourse is unproblematic, since he has already shown that every form is many beings and countless non-beings.

At 263D6–264B7 the philosopher is made to complete his proof that there are falsehoods by arguing that belief and perceptual judgment can be false. He in effect claims that they can be true or false, because they, like discourse, arise from thought, which is true or false. That his argument has this form is not immediately apparent, since he does not explicitly say that discourse arises from thought. Instead, he simply characterizes thought as unspoken discourse in the soul so that it being true or false may immediately be inferred. At 189E and 209D in the *Theaetetus* Plato makes it clear that spoken discourse is an expression of thought, and hence that the truth or falsity of discourse is derived from that of thought. The important point is that thought can be true or false because, like discourse, in it something is assumed to be a being in relation to a subject and what is assumed to be may be either a being or a non-being in relation to the subject. Thought differs from discourse in that its elements are not spoken sounds and it does not occur outside of the soul.

So the philosopher in effect argues that since thought is true or false, belief must also be true or false, since belief is a conclusion formed by thought in the soul that something is a being or a non-being in relation to a subject. In other words, belief is a mental affirmation or denial of the being of what is assumed in thought to be. At 236D10 the notion of seeming to be (*to dokein*), without being, was portrayed as suspect, and here Plato shows that it can be, since false belief (*doxa pseudē*), which expresses it, can be.

Finally, he argues that perceptual judgment can also be true or false, since it is belief of a certain sort. It is belief because it is the soul's affirmation or denial of what she assumes to be a being or a non-being. But since this belief arises on the basis of sensation (*di' aisthēseōs*, 264A4), it is the kind of perceptual belief that is given expression by the words, "it appears to be a being" (*phainetai*, 264B1) or "it appears to be a non-being."

Having answered the objection to non-being and the objection to being, which stood in the way of the definition of a sophist as a dealer in falsehoods and images, the philosopher then returns to the task of defining a sophist. In the process of answering these objections he has shown Theaetetus how dialectic can be used not only to expose the verbal tricks of the sophist, but also to establish non-being as a form, like being, motion, rest, the same and the other, of which all other forms partake.

Notes

[1] The theories the later Platonists attribute to Plato himself are more likely to represent what Plato himself believed that their interpretations of the theories attributed to him. However, many of their interpretations are clear implications of the views attributed to him.

[2] Theodorus is portrayed in the dialogue, *Theaetetus*, as the mathematics teacher of Theaetetus, whose beliefs about knowledge Socrates examines in the dialogue.

[3] In the dialogue named after him, (i) the young man, Theaetetus, is made to offer a definition of knowledge of the sort Plato thinks a sophist would present, a definition Plato thinks is based on the doctrine of universal flux held by Heraclitus and the maxim of Protagoras that man is the measure of all things, (ii) Socrates points out the faults of this sophistic definition and the two views upon which it is based, (iii) Plato then has Socrates present a number sophistic definitions of falsehood, but does not have Socrates refute them, most likely because he wanted his students to take up the task to refute them, and after setting aside a second definition, (iv) Theaetetus is made to present another definition based on a view of another sophist, Antisthenes, and is refuted. Hence, in the dialogue Plato rejects what he takes to be sophistic definitions of knowledge and raises the question of what nature is of falsehood. In the *Sophist*, the question of the nature of falsehood is again raised and answered, and the clues about how the nature of knowledge is to be defined are presented.

[4] Here and elsewhere I shall use, as the Greeks themselves did, masculine forms of expression, including pronouns, but not out of an intentional gender bias. "Wise person" is not, for instance, a good substitute for "wise man," which has, precisely, the connotations the Greek has. In the case of the exegesis of Greek philosophy, the various devices used to avoid masculine forms of expression usually distort the views being explained. In the case of pronouns, the commonly used devices used to avoid gender bias seem to be either to be too awkward in English or simply to change the bias toward the feminine.

[5] Most translators and commentators refer to the philosopher from Elea as "the Stranger." I refer to him as the philosopher because Plato clearly represents him as an accomplished philosopher.

[6] It is a common practice to capitalize "form" and "idea" when used to refer to what Plato calls a form or idea, and to capitalize the names of specific forms, so that "being" becomes "Being," "motion" becomes "Motion," etc. I shall not engage in this practice, which does not correspond to anything in the Greek. What ambiguities ensue reflect ambiguities in the Greek.

[7] The first place in which distinction between a universal present in a subject and a universal predicated of a subject occurs is in Aristotle's *Categories*. This does not mean, as most scholars believe, that the distinction is unknown to Plato. In fact, since it is likely that Aristotle's Categories was composed during the period in which he was a member of Plato's Academy, Plato surely knew of the distinction. Moreover, I believe, Aristotle introduces the distinction to help him identify a particular substance under the influence of Plato, who employed the distinction in the same way. This is one of my claims that most scholars of Plato's philosophy will deem controversial.

[8] In the *Metaphysics* Aristotle says that the Platonists believe that "there exists a form that has the same name as that which is said of many sensible substances as well as of sensible non-substances" (990b5-7). The sensible non-substances to which Aristotle refers are things like the four elements and the parts of substances, which he does not believe to be substances.

[9] In the translation of the *Sophist*, I translate *to on* as "being" rather than as "the being," which in

ordinary English is normally used to refer to a being previously mentioned. When *to on* is not used by Plato to refer to the form of being itself, but to what the form, being, is by its own nature, or to what something is that partakes of being, I translate it as "a being."

[10] *Ousia* is an abstract noun formed from the feminine form of the participle for *einai. On*, which is the neuter form of the participle, is implicit object of *estin* when *estin* is used by itself, as in sentences of the form, "X *estin*."

[11] See *Phaedo*, 99d• 100a.

[12] See *Phaedo*, 100c.

[13] In *Metaphysics*, Book XIV, Chapter 2, Aristotle calls these "being" and "non-being," which implies that he thinks that in the *Sophist* Plato is attempting to explain why there are many forms when he claims that non-being is a being. My account of what Plato uses this claim to do is based in part on what Aristotle says here.

[14] In the *Pheado*, one of the arguments used to establish the immortality of the human soul is based on its likeness to things that are incomposite. Such things are identified as forms and gods. The human soul, Plato believes, is itself an incomposite entity of this sort that possesses as its parts three different kinds of causal powers or faculties, which in the *Phaedrus* and the *Republic* Plato calls the intellect, spirit and appetite. A definition of a human soul would include mention of what these causal powers are.

[15] This is the method Plato believes can be used to establish the truth of his view that the cause of the many is the one. The difficulties faced by the doctrine that the many arise from the one were recognized by Plato. He expresses the main difficulty this view faces in the very first hypothesis about the one set out in the *Parmenides.* The main difficulty with the hypothesis that there is a one that is just one, he argues, is that nothing can be said of it at all. It cannot even be named. We need not attempt here to understand how Plato met such difficulties. What he does accomplish in the *Parmenides*, however, is to show that the way in which a form is one does not preclude it being many, since every form partakes of many other forms.

[16] See Aristotle's *Metaphysics*, I.9, at 990B13–14.

[17] The terms used by Parmenides, however, belonged to another dialect of Greek.

[18] In Chapter 9 of Book 1 of the *Physics*, Aristotle also attributes to Plato the view that because non-being can be, change is possible. But this notion of non-being is different from that Plato discusses in the Sophist. Plato apparently employed two different notions of non-being, one to explain how a plurality of being is possible and another to explain how change in possible.

[19] Antisthenes, a sophist, is reported to have asserted that there can be no falsehood. Plato, thinking that Protagoras' maxim, that man is the measure of all things, implies that there can be no falsehood, presents a more complicated account of the sophistic view that there can be no falsehood in the *Theaetetus* (187A10–201D4).

[20] In the case of "Being is a being" (*to on estin*), "is" (*estin*) is still being used as a copula, but in this case it expresses the notion that being is a being by its own nature, not the notion that it partakes of

being. Being is a being because by its own nature it possesses being, which is possessed by other things only if they partake of being.

[21] See note 4.

[22] How exactly sensible objects can be likenesses of immaterial forms is not clear. Perhaps the idea is that, just as a Picasso creates in his mind an image of a painting before it appears on a canvass, so the divine mind creates an image of a form in matter, or a Mozart creates in his min an image of a whole sonata before it is actually played. Although in these analogies, we believe that the images depend for their existence upon sense-perception, the images in the divine mind, Plato would say, do not. Such would be the difference between the human and divine imagination, the faculty of creating images of sensible objects.

[23] The mortal parts of our souls are created by the gods so that the thoughts formed in the immortal, intellective part of the soul can issue in bodily motion. See the *Timaeus*, 69E–72.

[24] This is how Plotinus interprets Plato's doctrine. Other interpretations are possible.

[25] Aristotle implies this when he objects to Plato's theory of forms in the *Metaphysics* I.9.

[26] Whether or not the Heracliteans and Empedocleans actually held the views Plato implies they held is not clear.

[27] In the fragments of Heraclitus what Plato here calls enmity Heraclitus calls the *logos*, fire, and god. The Stoic philosophy is a development of this theory, according to which there is present in matter, as a passive principle, an active material principle, which causes it to form into a world of sensible objects that possess individual and common characteristics and are caused to act upon or be acted upon by one another in accord with the laws of nature.

[28] In the *Theaetetus,* the Heracliteans are said to believe that a sensible object is a motion. But motion here is assumed to be the exercise of a causal power that is part of the nexus of causal powers whose exercise comprises the world of sense objects. The Heracliteans, it seems, did not think that these causal powers were fixed natures of underlying subjects. Plato surely knows that the Heracliteans said that the *logos* causes sensible objects to possess contrary natures.

[29] Compare the dream of Socrates in the *Theaetetus* (201D8–202D7) according to which there can be no account of simples (single-natured things), which can only be named, where an account involves applying many names to one thing. This is a view reported to have been held by Antisthenes, who also held that falsehoods are impossible. The view that falsehoods are impossible, however, seems to have been held by a number of different sophists.

[30] This statement of what a dialectician discerns is amenable to different interpretations. The interpretation given here is the simplest.

[31] Clearly, Plato must explain what the something else is when he refers to " something else" in his characterization of the difference between being and the other. However, since if there is *nothing* in relation to which something is other, it cannot be said that it is other. This is all Plato needs to say to make the argument work.

[32] I once again add "other than being" to his statement, since he has in fact only shown this conclusion to be true of each form other than being and because his next point will be that being itself is also both a being and a non-being.

[33] Here we would seem to have a Platonic account of how a being can come to be and how there can be many beings. Aristotle seems to attribute this account of how there can be many beings to Plato in *Metaphysics* XIV.2.

The Sophist

CHARACTERS IN THE DIALOGUE: THEODORUS (THEO.), SOCRATES (SOCR.), PHILOSOPHER (PHIL.), AND THEAETETUS (THEA.)

216 THEO. As is proper, Socrates, in keeping with the agreement we made yesterday,[1] we are here, and we bring with us this stranger from Elea who belongs to the circle of Parmenides and Zeno. He is a man proficient in philosophy.[2]

SOCR. Are you unaware, Theodorus, that you have not brought a stranger,
B but as Homer would say, a god? He says that the gods, especially the god of strangers, accompany persons who have a just sense of shame and that they keep watch on our lawful and unlawful actions.[3] So perhaps your companion, one of those superior beings, has come as a god of refutation to keep watch on our carelessness in discussions and to refute us.[4]

THEO. That is not the way of the stranger, Socrates; he is more moderate than those who zealously practice eristic. Although the man does not at all seem to me to be a god, he is godlike, since I speak of all philosophers as godlike.[5]

C SOCR. And rightly, my friend. But his kind is hardly any easier to discern than that of the god.[6] For these men, who do not pretend to be, but really are philosophers, appear in all sorts of shapes because of the ignorance of others and "keep returning to our cities," [7] watching from above the lives of those below; and to some they seem to be worth nothing, to others to be worth everything. Sometimes they appear to be philosophers, sometimes to be statesmen, sometimes to be sophists, and sometimes they may give the impression of being altogether mad. However, I should like to ask our stranger, if he is agreeable, what his countrymen think about this and what names they use.

217 THEO. Which names?

SOCR. "Sophist," "statesman" and "philosopher."

THEO. What special difficulty do you have about these names? What sort of thing about them did you intend to ask?

SOCR. It is this: did they think that all are [reducible to] one or two, or did they, since there are three names, distinguish three kinds and attach a name to each individually according to its kind?

THEO. I think he is, [like the gods,] without any envy[8] and will speak of these things. What should we say, stranger?

B PHIL. Just as you said, Theodorus. [Since, like the gods,] I am without envy, [I shall speak of these things;][9] nor is it difficult to report that they believe them to be three [in kind]. But it is no small or easy task to define clearly what each one of them is.

THEO. As chance would have it, Socrates, you have introduced for our discussion a question very like the one we happened to ask him before we arrived here. He made the very same excuses to us then as he is making to you now, even though he has been thoroughly instructed in these matters and has not forgotten them.

C SOCR. Then do not refuse us, stranger, a first favor we ask. Tell us this much: do you generally prefer to give a long speech by yourself and in this way to express what you want to point out to someone, or to ask questions,[10] as Parmenides once did when he presented a very fine set of arguments in my presence, when I was young and he was a very old man?

D PHIL. It is easier to ask questions of another, Socrates, when the one who responds is not bothersome and is easily guided;[11] otherwise, it is better to give a long speech by oneself.

SOCR. You can choose whomever you want to respond from among those present, for all will be compliant. But if you take my advice, you would choose one of the young men, Theaetetus here, or if you prefer, you may choose any of the others.

PHIL. Since this is our first meeting, Socrates, I am ashamed to present a long, drawn-out speech by myself or even to present one to another, as if I were presenting a fancy discourse, rather than having a discussion that
E advances little by little and word by word. For what is to be discussed now in fact happens to involve a very long discourse and not a discourse of the length one might expect from such a question. But not to grant a favor to you and to the others, especially since you spoke to me as you did, seems to me to be uncivilized and unsuitable behavior for a stranger. I am in complete accord with the choice of Theaetetus as my respondent, for I had a discussion with him earlier and you just called him to my attention.

218 THEA. Therefore, stranger, proceed in this way and you will have done a favor for all of us, just as Socrates said.

PHIL. Perhaps, Theaetetus, nothing remains to be said concerning these things; from now on, it seems, the argument will be directed to you. If then you should be bothered by the length of the task, do not blame me, but these companions of yours.

B THEA. I do not now think I shall quit the discussion for this reason. But if such a thing would happen, we shall invite the namesake of Socrates, the Socrates here who is my age and attends the gymnasium with me, for which reason he is not unaccustomed to working with me on many tasks.

PHIL. Well said; you will decide these things for yourself as the argument progresses. You and I must together first begin the investigation, as it seems to me, with a sophist, asking about his nature and making it clear by argument.[12] For now you and I have in common only his name. Each of us individually might understand the function by reference to which we call him by a name, but it is always and in every case necessary to agree
C about the thing itself by giving accounts rather than to agree only about a name without any account.[13] The sort of creature we have in mind to investigate, the sophist, is one whose nature is not the easiest to grasp. But for a long time it has been agreed by all that if great things are to be well-handled one must first practice on small things that are easier to grasp before handling the very greatest. So now, Theaetetus, since we are aware that the kind to which the sophist belongs is difficult to grasp and track down, I
D advise that we proceed in this way, to begin by practicing the method on something that is easier to grasp, unless you have another path to suggest similar to this.

THEA. I do not.

PHIL. Then do you wish us to pursue something of little consequence and try to make it an illustration of something more important?[14]

E THEA. I do.

PHIL. Then what shall we select that is well-known and insignificant, but no less capable of an account than something more significant? Let us take an angler as an example. Is he not known to all and not worth very much serious attention?[15]

THEA. It is as you say.

219 PHIL. And yet I hope he provides us with a method and an account that is suitable for our purposes.[16]

THEA. And that would be good.

PHIL. Come then, let us begin our pursuit of him in this way: tell me whether we shall suppose that he has a skill or art, or that he is without skill, but has some other power?[17]

THEA. Certainly not that he is without skill.

PHIL. However, of all arts, in general, there are two forms.

THEA. How so?

PHIL. Farming and whatever art attends to any mortal body, as well as any art that attends to what is constructed or molded, called an artifact, and the art of imitation, may rightly be called by one name.

B THEA. Why by one name? And by what name are they called?

PHIL. Whenever someone beings into being something that was not at first a being, we say, I suppose, that he who brings it into being produces it and that what is brought into being is produced.

THEA. Correct.

PHIL. All the arts we have just mentioned are efficacious for this reason.

THEA. Yes, they are.

PHIL. Thus we may bring them all together under one heading called skill in producing things.

C THEA. Let it be so.

PHIL. Again, after this there is the whole of the form of learning and the form of acquiring knowledge, as well as those of acquiring money, competing against others for things, and hunting for things. None of these produces anything, and some involve conquest by means of words or deeds things that are or have come to be, while others involve hindrance of conquest.[18] So I suppose that because it has all of these parts it would be best to call it an art of acquiring things.

THEA. Yes, that would be best.

D PHIL. Then, Theaetetus, if every art is either an art of acquiring things or of producing things, in which should we place the art of angling?[19]

THEA. Clearly, I suppose, in that of acquiring things.

PHIL. But are there not two forms of the art of acquiring things? The one pertains to exchange between two willing parties by means of gifts, wages, or purchases, and the other, since it involves conquest by word or deed, may as a whole be called the art of conquest.[20]

THEA. So it seems from what has been said.

PHIL. And must we not divide into two parts the art of conquest?

THEA. How?

E PHIL. By assuming that the part that as a whole is practiced out in the open is competing against others for things and the part that involves [the objects to be acquired being in] hiding is the sort of conquest generally called hunting.

THEA. Yes.

PHIL. However, it would be unreasonable not to divide into two parts the art of hunting.

THEA. Tell me how to do it.

PHIL. By distinguishing the hunting of lifeless things from the hunting of living things.

THEA. Surely, if there are both [kinds of hunting].

220 PHIL. How could there not be? The hunting of lifeless things we must leave without a name, except for some parts of the art of diving and other such

unimportant things, but the other, since it is the hunting of living creatures, we may call the art of animal hunting.[21]

THEA. Let us do so.

PHIL. And might not the form of animal hunting properly be called twofold? The one, the footed-animal kind, being the part concerned with the animal with feet and divisible into many forms and names, and the other, the water-animal hunting part, being as a whole concerned with the animal that swims?[22]

THEA. By all means.

B PHIL. However, of the kind that swim, one sort of creature is winged and another sort lives in the water.[23]

THEA. Of course.

PHIL. But every hunting of the winged[-creature] kind, I suppose, we call bird hunting.

THEA. We do.

PHIL. While the hunting of those that live in the water is generally called fishing.

THEA. Yes.

PHIL. Now should we not distinguish this kind of hunting into its two largest parts?

THEA. How are we to make the distinction?

PHIL. By reference to how the hunting is actually done, the one part being hunting with a trap and the other being hunting by striking.[24]

THEA. What do you mean? How do you distinguish each?

C PHIL. The one gets its name because whatever encloses something by surrounding it for the purpose of confinement is likely to be called a trap.

THEA. Certainly.

PHIL. And what else are we to call baskets, casting nets, nooses, and creels and the like but traps?

THEA. Nothing else.

PHIL. Therefore we shall call this the trapping part of fishing or some such thing.

THEA. Yes.

PHIL. Let us now refer to the other part of fishing, which differs from trapping and involves striking with hooks or three-pronged spears, by the single phrase, "hunting by striking." Or what better name, Theaetetus, could
D someone find for it?

THEA. Let's not be concerned about the name, since this one is sufficient.

PHIL. I think that the kind of hunting by striking that takes place at night by means of the light of a fire happens to be called fire lighting by hunters.

THEA. It certainly is.

PHIL. While the kind that takes place during the day they generally call hooking because their three-pronged spears also have hooks at the tips.[25]

E THEA. Yes, that is what they call it.

PHIL. Then of the hooking kind of hunting by striking, the part that takes place when the striking is downward from above is called, I believe, three-pronged spearing, since three-pronged spears are used in this way.[26]

THEA. Some say this, at least.

PHIL. Then there remains yet only one form of which to speak.

THEA. What is that?

221 PHIL. The form in which the striking is in the contrary direction. The fish are hooked not in any chance part of their body, as happens with three-pronged spears, but always in the head or mouth, and are pulled up from below in the contrary direction by a fishing rod or cane. By what name should we say this is called, Theaetetus?

THEA. I think we have now completed the very task we previously set out for ourselves as necessary.

PHIL. Therefore, not only have you and I now agreed about the name of the
B angling art, but also we have an adequate grasp of the account of its very function. For of skill as a whole, half was that in acquiring things; of skill in acquiring things, half was acquiring them by conquest; half of acquiring them by conquest was hunting; half of hunting was animal hunting; half of animal hunting was water-animal hunting; half of water-animal hunting was the division below it as a whole, fishing; half of fishing was the striking part; and half of the striking part was hooking. And of hooking the half that was concerned with striking by pulling up from below and whose name was derived from this action, was just now discovered to be called angling.

C THEA. So that has been made absolutely and sufficiently clear.

PHIL. Come then, let us set out to discover what the sophist is according to this paradigm.

THEA. By all means.

PHIL. The first question was whether we must suppose that the angler has an art or is unskilled.[27]

THEA. It was.

PHIL. And now shall we suppose, Theaetetus, that this one is unskilled or that he is in every way truly a sophist?

D THEA. He is not at all unskilled, for I understand you to mean that one who is called "unskilled" is without any skill at all.

PHIL. So it seems that we must suppose that he has some sort of art.[28]

THEA. But what sort of art can it be?

PHIL. By the gods! Have we failed to notice that these men are of the same kind?[29]

THEA. Which men?

PHIL. The angler and the sophist.

THEA. How?

PHIL. Both appear to me to be hunters of a sort.

E THEA. What does the second hunt? For we have discussed the first.

PHIL. I believe we just now divided all things hunted into two divisions, the swimming-animal part and the footed-animal part.

THEA. Yes.

PHIL. The one, which concerned those that live in the water and swim, we discussed; the other we left undivided, saying that it is of many forms.

222 THEA. Certainly.

PHIL. So up to that point, the sophist and the angler together are made to proceed from the art of acquiring things.

THEA. At least it seems so.

PHIL. They part company at the art of animal hunting; an angler, it seems, goes to the sea, rivers, and lakes to hunt the animals in them.

THEA. To be sure.

PHIL. But the sophist goes to the dry land and to rivers of a different sort, rivers of wealth and youth, as it were, bounteous meadows, with the intention of conquering the creatures in them.

B THEA. What do you mean?

PHIL. From footed-animal hunting there are generated two most extensive parts of a certain sort.

THEA. Of what sort is each?

PHIL. The one part is the hunting of tame animals and the other is the hunting of wild animals.

THEA. Can there be any hunting of tame animals?

PHIL. There can, at least if a human being is a tame animal. But assume what you want, either that there is no tame animal, that some other animal is tame but a human being is wild, or again that although a human being is tame, there is no hunting of a human being. Determine for us which of these assumptions you want to make.[30]

C THEA. Well, stranger, I believe that we are tame animals and say that there is the hunting of human beings.[31]

PHIL. Then let us say that the art of tame animal hunting is also twofold.

THEA. How should we distinguish them?

PHIL. By defining piracy, kidnapping, tyranny, and the whole of the art of war, one and all, as hunting by forceful action.

THEA. Good.

PHIL. And the other kind we distinguish by calling [the arts of] forensic speech, public speaking and private conversation, one and all, [since used to acquire things], by the name of a single art, the art of persuasion.[32]

D THEA. Right.

PHIL. And of the art of [hunting by the use of] persuasion we should say there are two kinds.

THEA. What are they?

PHIL. One of the two comes to be in private gatherings and the other in public.[33]

THEA. Yes, a form of each comes to be.

PHIL. Then again, one part of the art of hunting in private gatherings involves being paid, and the other involves bringing gifts.[34]

THEA. I do not understand.

PHIL. So it seems that you have not yet noticed how lovers hunt.

THEA. What have I not noticed?

E PHIL. And that they also present gifts to those they hunt.

THEA. Very true.

PHIL. Then let this be a form of the lovers' art.[35]

THEA. Certainly.

PHIL. And that part of the art [of hunting in private gatherings by the use of persuasive words] that involves being paid, which includes the use of ingratiating conversation, with pleasure as bait, and the wage set is one's own subsistence, I think, we would all say is the art of flattery or of pleasure-giving.

223 THEA. Certainly.

PHIL. But the part that includes the claim that conversation is held for the sake of virtue, and the wage set is cash, does not this kind deserve to be called by another name?[36]

THEA. Certainly.

PHIL. And what is this name? Try to tell me what it is.

THEA. It is obvious. For we seem to me to have come upon [the art of] the sophist. So in using this word, I believe that I would be calling him by his right name.

B PHIL. Then, according to the present account, Theaetetus, it seems that [the art of] hunting young men of wealth and reputation, which is generated from

the arts of acquiring things, appropriating them [or conquering them], hunting, animal hunting, hunting of animals living on dry land [or footed-animals], tame animal hunting, hunting of humans, hunting in private gatherings, exchanging for money the appearance of educating them, must be called sophistry.[37]
THEA. By all means.
PHIL. Yet, we may also look for his kind in another way. For what is now being sought is not something that pertains to a simple, but to an art that is
C very complex. For in what we said before[38] the impression is given that it is not what we are now saying it is, but some other kind.
THEA. How?
PHIL. The form of the art of acquiring things, I believe, was twofold, one part being hunting and the other being exchange.
THEA. Yes, it was.
PHIL. We may now say that there are two forms of exchange, that of the giving and receiving of gifts and that of buying and selling.
THEA. Let it be so.
PHIL. And skill in buying and selling, again, we shall say is divisible into two parts.
D THEA. How shall we divide it?
PHIL. By distinguishing the selling of one's own work from exchange of the sort in which the works of others are exchanged.
THEA. Certainly.
PHIL. Well, then. Is not exchange that occurs within the city and is virtually one half of skill in exchange to be called skill in retailing?
THEA. It is.
PHIL. Is the part in which exchange takes place from one city to another by buying and selling to be called commerce?
THEA. Of course.
E PHIL. Are we not aware that one part of skill in commerce exchanges for money whatever the body takes in as nourishment and uses, and the other part exchanges for money whatever the soul takes in as nourishment and uses?
THEA. What do you mean by this?
PHIL. Perhaps we are unfamiliar with the part concerning the soul, since I assume that we understand the other part.
THEA. Yes.
224 PHIL. Let us then say that any education in the arts that is on any occasion bought in one city and brought to another elsewhere to be sold, including [education in] painting, wonder-working, and the many other things brought

and sold for the sake of either the diversion of the soul or its serious activities, enables the one who brings and sells them, no less than the one who sells food and drink, to be correctly called a merchant.

THEA. Very true.

B PHIL. Then will you not apply the same name to him who buys up learning in one city and exchanges it for money in another city?

THEA. Most certainly.

PHIL. Then should not one part of this art of merchandising for the soul rightly be called the art of putting on a show [of his learning for money] and the other part be called by a name no less ridiculous than "soul-merchandising"? But must not this sale of things to be learned have applied to it a name akin to its activity?

THEA. By all means.

C PHIL. Then the part of this skill in selling learning, the one that concerns learning other arts, must be called by one name, and the part that concerns virtue, must be called by another.

THEA. Of course.

PHIL. "Skill-selling" would be appropriate for one part. Now you must try to name the other.

THEA. What other name could one give more appropriate than "sophistry," the name of the very kind we are now seeking?

PHIL. No other. Come now, let us bring this kind together by saying that sophistry appears in a second way, as the selling of virtue, which is part of
D the arts of acquiring things, exchange, buying and selling, and commerce that is soul-merchandising concerned with discourses and learning.

THEA. Very well.

PHIL. Thirdly, I think that even if someone should remain in his city and make his living either by buying learning or by making them himself in order to sell them, you would call his art by no other name than the very one used just now.

THEA. Why would I not do so?

PHIL. Therefore, as it seems, you will always apply the term "sophistry" to
E that part of the art of acquiring things that is exchange through buying and selling, regardless whether of goods made by another or by oneself, whenever the kind deals with selling things to be learned.

THEA. Necessarily, since one must follow the account.

PHIL. Then let us continue by examining whether in that case the kind we are pursuing is like something of the following sort.

225 THEA. Of what sort?

PHIL. A part of the art of acquiring things for us was the art of competing with others.

THEA. It was.

PHIL. Then we shall not go wrong by dividing this into two.

THEA. Tell me how.

PHIL. By supposing that one part pertains to contests and the other to combat.

THEA. True.

PHIL. Then it is fitting and appropriate to suppose that we call the part of the art of combat that involves bodily interaction by some such name as the "violent" part.

THEA. Yes.

PHIL. But the part that involves verbal interaction, Theaetetus, what else should someone call it but the "argumentative" kind?

B THEA. Nothing else.

PHIL. And we must suppose that the argumentative part is twofold.

THEA. How?

PHIL. The part of argumentation that occurs in public life involves long discourses opposed to one another and concerns things that are just or unjust is the judicial kind.

THEA. Yes.

PHIL. Are we accustomed to calling anything but disputation the part that occurs in the private sector and is cut up into bits by question and answers?

THEA. Nothing else.

PHIL. The part of disputation that concerns argumentation about matters of everyday life, but occurs informally and unskillfully, may be supposed to be one form, since our account recognizes it is as different. But it is not
C worth a name now.

THEA. True, for it has been divided into parts too small and diverse.

PHIL. But the part that concerns skillful argumentation about things that are in themselves just and unjust, as well as about other things in general, we are accustomed to calling this the "eristic" kind of disputation, are we not?

THEA. Certainly.

D PHIL. One part of the eristic kind of disputation pertains to the wasting of money, the other to the making of money.

THEA. Absolutely.

PHIL. Then let us try to call each by its rightful name.

THEA. Indeed we must.

PHIL. But I think that the part of eristic that gives rise to carelessness in one's own affairs because of the enjoyment of engaging in this activity, and involves discourse that the many who hear it do not enjoy, is, in my opinion, to be called nothing other than babbling.

THEA. Yes, it is called something like that.

E PHIL. So it is now your turn to try to explain its contrary, the part that pertains to the making of money from eristic in the private sector.

THEA. What else could one say, if one wants to avoid error, except that a sophist, that wondrous fellow whom we have been seeking, has returned for the fourth time?

226 PHIL. The present argument shows, as it seems, that [the art of] a sophist is nothing but the money-making kind of eristic art, which is an art of disputation, combat, competing with others, and acquiring things.

THEA. Exactly.

PHIL. So do you see how true it is to say that the animal we seek is complex, and, as the saying goes, is not to be captured with one hand.

THEA. Then we must use both.

B PHIL. And so we must do the best we can by following his trail in some such way as this: tell me, do we call some things by the names used by household servants?[39]

THEA. Yes, many, but about what sorts of things are you asking?

PHIL. We speak of such things as straining, winnowing, and filtering.

THEA. Certainly.

PHIL. And in addition to these, we know of carding, combing, warping, and a thousand other such activities present in the arts.

C THEA. What sort of thing did you want to make clear by putting forward and asking about all of these examples?

PHIL. All of the activities that have been mentioned, I suppose, are said to involve dividing things.

THEA. Yes.

PHIL. Then in accord with my theory that there is one art for all of these, we shall require one name for it.

THEA. And what shall we call it?

PHIL. The art of separation.

THEA. Let it be so.

PHIL. Again, examine whether we can somehow discern two forms of this.

THEA. You seem to me to be requiring a quick examination.

D PHIL. But at least among the separating activities mentioned, some were a dividing of the worse from the better and the others were a dividing of like from like.

THEA. What you have said now certainly seems to be so.

PHIL. I do not know a name for the one kind of separation, but I do for the other in which the better is kept and the worse is rejected.

THEA. Tell me what it is.

PHIL. Every separation of that sort, as I understand it, is generally called a purification.

THEA. And so it is.

E PHIL. And does not purification, again, have a twofold form about which
everyone should see?

THEA. Perhaps so, given enough time, but I do not see it now.

PHIL. Well, in fact there are many forms of bodily purifications that may properly be embraced by one name.

THEA. What are they and what is the name?

PHIL. The forms of bodily purification of living creatures are those in which
things inside their bodies are purged when correctly separated out by the arts
227 of gymnastics and medicine and insignificant things outside their bodies are
purged by separations provided by the art of the bath man. And the forms of
the purification of lifeless bodies are those with which the laundering arts,
and, in general, the decorative arts are concerned having many subdivisions
whose names seem to be ridiculous.

THEA. Very much so.

PHIL. Absolutely, Theaetetus. But then, in the pursuit of accounts, the
sponging art is just as important as that of dispensing drugs, neither more nor
less, even though in one case the benefit from the purification may be small
and in the other case it may be great. For the pursuit is an attempt to
understand what is and is not akin in all the arts for the sake of gaining
insight. It values all of them equally in this respect. It does not regard some
B things that are like one another as more ridiculous than others. It does not at
all think that making the art of hunting clear by reference to the general's art
rather than by reference to the art of the exterminator is something more
dignified, but that it is for the most part pretentious. And in particular now, in
relation to your question about what name we shall give to all of these
powers that are taken to purge both living and lifeless bodies, it makes no
difference to this pursuit what sort of name sounds best. Just let it be distinct
C from the name of the purifications of the soul and unite everything that
purges anything else. For the pursuit has now attempted to separate
purification pertinent to thought from the rest, if we understand its purpose.

THEA. But I do understand its purpose, and I agree that there are two forms of purification; one form concerns the soul and is distinct from that which concerns the body.

D PHIL. Excellent. Listen to what I say next and try again to divide into two the form just mentioned.

THEA. I shall try to divide it for you in accord with whatever you suggest.

PHIL. Do we say that wickedness in the soul is something other than virtue?

THEA. Of course.

PHIL. And purification was the retaining of the latter and expulsion of whatever is bad anywhere.

THEA. It was.

PHIL. Therefore, whenever we should discover a case of vice being removed from soul, we shall, if we are to speak correctly, call it a purification.

THEA. We shall.

PHIL. We must say that two forms of vice concern the soul.

THEA. What are they?

PHIL. The one is like disease in the body, the other like its coming to be ugly.

228 THEA. I do not understand.

PHIL. Perhaps you do not think that disease and discord are the same?

THEA. Again, I do not know what answer I should give to this.

PHIL. Is it because you think that discord is something other than what is united by nature being dissolved because of some division?

THEA. No.

PHIL. But is ugliness anything else than the kind of disproportion that is always hard to look at?

B THEA. Nothing else.

PHIL. Do we not see in the soul of those who are in a sorry condition that beliefs disagree with appetites, anger with pleasures, reason with pains, and all of these with one another?

THEA. Very much so.

PHIL. Yet all of them must agree.

THEA. Of course.

PHIL. Therefore we shall speak correctly if we say that wickedness is discord or disease of the soul.

THEA. Absolutely.

C PHIL. When things partaking of motion and aiming at some target they attempt to hit go astray each time the attempt is made, shall we say that this occurs by reason of their proportion to one another, or that, on the contrary, it occurs by reason of their disproportion?

THEA. Clearly by reason of their disproportion.

PHIL. But yet we know that no soul is ignorant of anything voluntarily.

THEA. We certainly do.

PHIL. Yet ignorance is nothing other than a disorder of a soul that aims at truth when understanding has gone astray.

THEA. By all means.

D PHIL. Therefore, we must suppose that a soul without understanding is ugly and ill-proportioned.

THEA. It seems so.

PHIL. Indeed, there are these two kinds of vices in the soul; one is called wickedness by the many and is very clearly a disease of the soul.

THEA. Yes.

PHIL. The other they call ignorance, but are not inclined to agree that it is a vice when it comes to be only in the soul.

E THEA. I must agree completely, though I doubted it when you said it just now, that there are two kinds of vice in the soul. And we must believe that cowardice, intemperance, and injustice are, as a whole, a disease in us, and we must suppose that our state of widespread and manifold ignorance is ugliness in us.

PHIL. Are there not two arts that are concerned with these two states when in the body?

THEA. What are they?

229 PHIL. Gymnastics, which is concerned with ugliness, and medicine, which is concerned with disease.

THEA. It seems so.

PHIL. So of all the arts is not the art of correction the one most closely akin to justice and especially concerned with insolence, injustice, and cowardice?

THEA. In my human opinion, so to speak, that is at least likely.

PHIL. And what about ignorance as a whole? No art concerned with correcting it would be more proper to cite than that of instruction, is there?

THEA. None at all.

PHIL. Then should we say that there is just one kind of instruction or
B more, two of which are the most important? Think.

THEA. I am.

PHIL. I think we would find out most quickly in the following way.

THEA. How?

PHIL. By seeing whether ignorance itself somehow admits of a division in the middle. For if it happens to be twofold, it is clear that instruction must have two parts, one for each kind of ignorance.

THEA. Well, is what we seek now clear to you somehow?

C PHIL. I believe, at least, that I see an extensive and unbearable form of ignorance that is separate and is to be weighed against all of its other parts together.

THEA. What is it?

PHIL. To think one knows something when he does not. Because of this, it seems, all of our errors in thought arise.

THEA. True.

PHIL. Furthermore, I think that the name "stupidity" is applied to this kind of ignorance alone.

THEA. Certainly.

PHIL. Then what should we call that part of the art of instruction that frees us from this ignorance?

D THEA. I think, stranger, that the other kind of instruction concerns craftsmanship, while this kind we here call education.

PHIL. And so it is, Theaetetus, by virtually all Greeks. But we must still investigate whether education as a whole is indivisible or allows of some division worth naming.

THEA. Then we must investigate.

PHIL. It seems to me that this too is split somewhere.

THEA. On what basis?

PHIL. One method of the art of instruction by means of discourse seems to be rougher, the other part of it is smoother.

THEA. What do we call each of these?

E PHIL. The one was venerated by our fathers and especially used by them to educate their sons, and used by many still now, when their sons make mistakes, sometimes being angry and sometimes advising them gently. So in general, one would be most correct in calling it the art of admonition.

THEA. It is so.

PHIL. On the other hand, some think on the basis of argument that it is right to maintain that all stupidity is involuntary, that he who thinks of himself
230 as wise would never be willing to learn the things about which he thinks he is clever, and that the form of education called admonition accomplishes little after a lot of hard work.

THEA. They are right.

PHIL. So they set about in another way to cast out this belief.

THEA. In what way?

B PHIL. They ask questions about things about which someone thinks he is saying something when he is saying nothing. Then they easily assess the beliefs of those in error, gather them in their arguments into the same place, set them beside one another, and then having done this, they demonstrate that

the beliefs are contrary to one another at the same time, concerning the same things, in relation to the same things, and in the same way. Those who realize this become angry with themselves, but patient with others. In this
C way they are freed from their pompous and dogmatic beliefs about them selves in a way that is a most pleasant experience for those who listen and permanently affects those whose souls are purged. For, my boy, those who purge them think like the physicians of the body who believe that the body cannot benefit from the nourishment given to it until someone eliminates the impediments within it. They think the same thing about the soul, that
D she will not benefit from the learning given to her until a questioner puts the person questioned to shame, and removes the beliefs that impede learning and purge him, so that he believes himself to know only as much as he knows and no more.

THEA. This, at any rate, is the best and most sober disposition.

PHIL. So for all these reasons, Theaetetus, we must say that questioning is the greatest and most effective of all purgations. We must also think that one who has not been questioned, even if he should be the great king himself, has not been purged of error about the most important matters, so he is uneducated and ugly in matters in which he who is really to be
E happy ought to be most pure and beautiful.

PHIL. Then what shall we call those who employ this art? For I am afraid to call them sophists.

231 THEA. Why?

PHIL. Because we could be paying them too great an honor.

THEA. But the things just said of them are like [things said of] someone of this sort.

PHIL. And a wolf, the wildest of creatures, is like a dog, the tamest. He who would be cautious must always be on guard most especially against likenesses, since the kind [to which they belong] is most slippery. Let them, nonetheless, be [sophists], since I think there will be no arguments about terms of little importance when persons are sufficiently on their guard.

B THEA. It is not likely.

PHIL. Then let a part of the art of separating things be the purification art, and of the purification art let the part that concerns the soul be separated off. Of this, let a part be the art of instruction, and of the art of instruction let a part be education. And let us say that within education, the refutation of the empty appearance of wisdom that has shown itself in the present discussion is nothing other than a sophistry of noble lineage.

C THEA. Let it be so called. But because he has appeared to be many things, I am perplexed about what we should say a sophist really is if we are to speak confidently and to affirm the truth.

PHIL. It is natural that you are perplexed. But you must consider that the sophist by now is very perplexed about how he will contrive to evade our account. For it is rightly said that it is not easy to escape all methods of capture. So now, especially, we should set out after him.

THEA. Well said.

PHIL. First then, let us stop to catch our breath, and while we are resting let
D us review the many ways in which the sophist has appeared. I believe that we first found him to be a paid hunter of young wealthy men.

THEA. Yes.

PHIL. Secondly, he appeared as a kind of merchant of learning for the soul.

THEA. Certainly.

PHIL. Thirdly, did he not appear as a retailer of these same things?

THEA. Yes, and fourthly he was for us one who sells his own learning.

PHIL. You remember correctly. I will try to remember how he appeared the
E fifth time. He was the kind of athlete who competes with words and makes the eristic art his own.

THEA. So he was.

PHIL. His sixth appearance was open to argument, but we did agree to suppose that the sophist was a purifier of beliefs that impede the soul's acquisition of knowledge.

THEA. Exactly.

232 PHIL. So do you understand that when someone appears to have knowledge of many things, but is called after the name of a single art, this impression is not sound? And is it not clear that he who has this impression about any art cannot see in it what it is to which all of these forms of skill pertain, for which reason he calls one who possesses them by many names instead of one?

THEA. This may very well be the way it happens.

B PHIL. Then we should not out of laziness let this happen in our inquiry. Rather, let us begin by taking up something we said about the sophist, since there was one thing that seemed to me in particular to bring him out into the open.

THEA. What was it?

PHIL. I believe we said he was skillful in disputation.

THEA. Yes.

PHIL. And did we not say that he becomes a teacher of this same thing to others?

THEA. Certainly.

PHIL. Then let us inquire into this: about what subject do such persons say they make others skillful in disputation? Let us begin our examination in this way: do they make their students qualified to dispute about things divine and unseen by the many?

C THEA. At least it is said that they do this.

PHIL. And what about things seen on earth and in the heavens and things of that sort?

THEA. Yes.

PHIL. Furthermore, in private gatherings, whenever something is said about the coming to be or being of all things, do we understand that they are clever at speaking against it and that they make others able to do so as well?

THEA. Absolutely.

D PHIL. And again, what about laws and all of the affairs of state? Do they not promise to make their students skilled in argument about these things?

THEA. Virtually no one would converse with them if they did not make this promise.

PHIL. Moreover, how to speak against a practitioner of any and every art has been set down in writing and is available to anyone wanting to acquire the skill.

THEA. You appear to me to be speaking of the writings of Protagoras about wrestling and the other arts.

PHIL. And, young man, of the writings of many others! But does not the art
E of disputation, to summarize, seem to be a power of the sort sufficient to enable one to argue about everything?

THEA. At least it appears to omit virtually nothing.

PHIL. By the gods, my boy, do you think this is possible? For perhaps you young people can see this more clearly than those of us whose vision is dimmer.

233 THEA. See what? What exactly are you saying we are to see? For I do not think I understand what you are now asking.

PHIL. I was asking whether anyone can possibly know everything.

THEA. Were that so, stranger, our kind would be blessed.

PHIL. Then how could it ever be possible for someone without knowledge to speak against one with knowledge and say something sound?

THEA. It is not possible at all.

PHIL. Then what could the marvelous power of sophistry be?

THEA. In what way is their power marvelous?

B PHIL. In the way they are able to produce in the young the belief that they themselves exceed all others in being wise in everything. For it is clear that if they were not good at disputation or did not seem to the young to be good, or even if, while appearing to be good at disputation, they seemed to be in no way more intelligent because of their argumentation, virtually no one, as you said, would want to give them money to become learned in these same things.

THEA. Virtually no one.

PHIL. But as it is, they want to do this?

THEA. Very much so.

C PHIL. For they seem, I think, to have knowledge of these things about which they dispute.

THEA. Certainly.

PHIL. And we said that they dispute about everything?

THEA. Yes.

PHIL. Therefore, they appear wise in all things to their students.

THEA. Yes.

PHIL. Yet they are not, since this appeared to be impossible.

THEA. How could it be otherwise?

PHIL. Therefore the sophist has reappeared having a kind of reputed knowledge of everything, but not having the truth.

D THEA. Absolutely. What has just now been said is probably the most correct thing said about the sophists.

PHIL. Then let us work with a clearer example.

THEA. What sort of example?

PHIL. The example is as follows; do your best to answer my question by paying careful attention to it.

THEA. What is your question?

PHIL. If someone should say that he knows not how to speak and to dispute about everything, but how to produce or accomplish by a single art all things . . .

E THEA. All things! What do you mean?

PHIL. Right off you fail to comprehend the point of what I have said, since you apparently do not understand "all things."

THEA. No, I do not.

PHIL. By "all things" I mean you and me, and besides us, trees and other living beings.

THEA. What do you mean?

PHIL. [I mean that] if someone should say that he is going to produce you and me and all other living things . . .

THEA. But what sort of thing could he mean by "produce?" For you are not
234 speaking of a farmer, since you said he is a producer of living beings.

PHIL. I say that he is, and in addition, that he is a producer of sea and earth, heaven and gods, and all other things. And then, having produced each of them quickly, he gives them up for very little money.

THEA. You are speaking of a game.

PHIL. And what about this? Should we not consider it a game when someone says that he knows all things and that for a small fee he would quickly teach what he knows to another?

THEA. We certainly should.

PHIL. And do you know of a form of game more skillful or more pleasing than imitation?

B THEA. Not at all. For by having one form embrace all things, you are speaking of a very comprehensive and most complex form.

PHIL. And so, I suppose, we recognize that one who promises to be able to produce all things by means of a single art, fashions, by means of the painters' art, imitations called by the same names by which the beings imitated are called, and that he will be able, when he shows his pictures from a distance to foolish young children, to deceive them into thinking that he is in fact most competent to carry out whatever he should want to do.

C THEA. Of course.

PHIL. What then? Should we not expect that there to be another art [of imitation] that employs words? An art in which they can be employed to cast a spell on the ears of the young, who stand far away from the truth of things, by showing them spoken images of all things? So that what is said is made to seem to be true and that the one who speaks is made to seem to possess the greatest wisdom concerning all things?

D THEA. Why should there not be another art [of imitation] of this sort?

PHIL. Therefore, Theaetetus, must not the many who heard these things change the beliefs so acquired after a sufficient amount of time has passed when they have matured and by experience are forced to make direct contact with things to which circumstances have brought them near? Does it not follow that what once seemed to them to be great now seems small, what
E once seemed easy now seems difficult, and that all the semblances formed by words have been entirely overturned by things they encounter by their actions?

THEA. It does so, at least in the judgment of someone my age. But I think that I am one of those who still "stand far away" from the truth of things.

PHIL. Therefore, all of us here shall continue to try to bring you as near as possible to the truth without the experiences [that force others to make contact with it]. Therefore, tell me this about the sophist. Is it now clear that

235 he is a magician who makes images of beings? Or are we still in doubt whether he does in truth possess knowledge of all the things about which he seems to be able to dispute?

THEA. How could he [possess such knowledge], stranger? It is already reasonably clear from what has been said that he is one who plays a game.

PHIL. So we should suppose that he is a magician and maker of images.

THEA. How could we not make that supposition?

PHIL. Come on, then! Our task now is not to let our prey get away. For we
B have just about encircled him by a net composed of the verbal instruments [of knowledge] of such things. So he shall not escape this, at least.

THEA. Escape what?

PHIL. That he be [classified as] a kind of maker of things wondrous.

THEA. This is also what he seems to me to be.

PHIL. Then it seems that we may proceed immediately to divide the art of image-making, and upon going down into it, if the sophist should be lying in wait for us, take hold of him by the authority of the account we have made
C our king, and when we hand him over, announce the capture. But if he should take cover somewhere in the parts of [the art of] imitation, we shall follow him by always dividing the part that receives him, until he should be taken. Neither this nor any other kind will ever boast of its escape from the method of those capable of pursuing it in this way in each and every case.

THEA. You are right to say that things should be done in this way.

D PHIL. In accord with the aforementioned way of dividing [the art] I now also seem to see two forms of the art of imitation. But I do not yet seem to be able to discern in which of the two forms the idea we seek happens to be.

THEA. Well, anyhow, first distinguish them for us and tell us what the two are.

PHIL. Included in the art of imitation, I see. First of all, the art of making likenesses. The special character of this art is that someone produces an imitation that agrees with the proportions of its original in length, breadth,
E and depth, and also gives the appropriate colors to each [of its parts].

THEA. But do not all who imitate something attempt to do this?

PHIL. Not those, I suppose, who sculpt or paint something of great size. For if they should transfer the real proportions of their beautiful [originals], you know that the upper parts would appear smaller and the bottom parts larger than need be because we see the former from far away and the latter from close up.

236 THEA. Very true.

PHIL. Therefore, since the artists are unconcerned about what is true, they work into their images not the actual proportions [of the originals] but those that appear to be beautiful, do they not?

THEA. Certainly.

B PHIL. Therefore, is it not correct to call the other one a likeness, since it is like the original?

THEA. Yes.

PHIL. And the part of the art of imitation concerned with it we should call the art of likeness-making, as we did before.

THEA. We should.

PHIL. But what of a work that appears to be like the beautiful [original] because not seen from the right perspective, but would not appear to be like it if someone were able properly to see something of such a size? What do we call it? Do we not call it a semblance because it appears to be a likeness, but is not?

THEA. We do.

PHIL. And is not this a very large part of both painting and the art of imitation as a whole?

C THEA. Certainly.

PHIL. And surely would we not be most correct to call an art in which a semblance rather than a likeness is produced the art of semblance-making?

THEA. Very much so.

PHIL. These are then the two forms of the art of image-making I mentioned, the arts of likeness-making and of semblance-making.

THEA. True.

PHIL. I am still not able to see clearly that about which I was uncertain earlier, where the sophist is to be put. But he is in fact a wondrous fellow and very difficult to discern. For now he has very well and cleverly taken refuge
D in a form in which he is difficult to track down.

THEA. It seems he has.

PHIL. Are you agreeing [that the form is difficult to track down] because you are familiar with it, or is it that something like an impulse has drawn you into quick agreement because you have been conditioned by the discussion [to agree]?

THEA. What do you mean? Why did you say this?

PHIL. My dear friend, we really are engaging in a very difficult inquiry. For
E this appearing to be and seeming to be, without being, and saying things, but things not true, all such things have always been and still are utterly perplexing. For it is very difficult, Theaetetus, to see how a person can say or believe that there really are falsehoods without being caught up in a

statement contrary to itself.

237 THEA. Why is it so difficult?

PHIL. This statement is based on the daring hypothesis that a non-being is a being, since in no other way would a falsehood become a being. When we were children, my boy, Parmenides the Great began to object to this [hypothesis] and continued to do so to the end of his life both in prose and in verse:

> "Never let it prevail that non-beings are beings.
> In pursuit of the truth keep your thought from this path."

B This is what he said, and of all his theories, it is especially this one that would be clarified by being put to the test [of reason]. So let us begin, if it makes no difference to you, by examining this theory.

THEA. As far as I am concerned, you may do as you please. As for the theory, you must decide for yourself how it will best be examined; so continue on and lead me along this same path.

PHIL. This will be done. Tell me, do we dare to speak of a non-being?

THEA. Why not?

PHIL. Then, if anyone should listen to, and consider without being contentious, or as a joke, the question, "To what should this name, '*non*-being,' be
C applied?," how do we think that he would answer? To what or to what kind of thing will he apply it? What will he show to one who asks the question?

THEA. The question is difficult; I may say in fairness that it is wholly unanswerable for someone like me.

PHIL. But one thing seems clear [about Parmenides' theory]: we should not apply "non-being" to any being.

THEA. Certainly not.

PHIL. And if it cannot be applied to a being, neither would we be correct to apply it to something.

THEA. Why?

D PHIL. It is obvious to us, I assume, that we always use this "something" to refer to a being. For it is impossible to speak of this in isolation, as if naked and stripped away from all beings, is it not?

THEA. It is impossible.

PHIL. Looking at the matter in this way, then, do you grant me that he who speaks of something must be speaking of something that is one?

THEA. I do.

PHIL. You will say, in fact, that "something" in its singular form is a sign of one thing, in its dual form, a sign of a pair of things, and in its plural form, a sign of many things.

THEA. Of course.

E PHIL. So it follows necessarily that he who speaks of non-something is speaking of *non*-one.[40]

THEA. Necessarily.

PHIL. Then we should not agree that someone can speak of something and also be speaking of a non-one. Instead, should we not say that he who tries to speak of a non-being does not speak at all?[41]

THEA. This would seem to be the very purpose of the statement [Parmenides made] of the difficulty [about non-being].

238 PHIL. You mean that it is [the problem about non-being that is] important; but it is not. For, my friend, the first and greatest of the problems remains, since it affects the very first principle upon which his statement [of the problem] depends.[42]

THEA. What are you saying? Do not hesitate to tell me.

PHIL. To a being may be added some other being.

THEA. No doubt.

PHIL. But can we say that a being could ever be added to a non-being?

THEA. How could we?

PHIL. Now we assume that number, as a whole, is among beings.

B THEA. If anything else is assumed to be a being, number is too.

PHIL. Then let us not even attempt to add the one or many in number to non-being.

THEA. It does seem that the argument implies that we would be mistaken to make the attempt.

PHIL. Then how could anyone at all, without reference to number, express in speech, or even grasp in thought, non-beings or non-being?

THEA. Tell me how.

C PHIL. Whenever we speak of non-beings, are we not attempting to add [to non-being] the many in number?

THEA. Yes, of course.

PHIL. Again, whenever we speak of a non-being, are we not attempting to add [to non-being] the one in number?

THEA. Most assuredly.

PHIL. We are speaking neither rightly nor correctly when we attempt to attach a being to a non-being.

THEA. Quite true.

PHIL. Do you then understand that there can be no correct way to express in speech or to speak or think of non-being itself by itself, and that it cannot be thought, be given a name, be expressed in speech, or have an account?

THEA. I certainly do.

D PHIL. Then I was mistaken just now when I spoke of the greatest difficulty in speaking about it.

THEA. Do we have a still greater one to discuss?

PHIL. Why, young man, do you not understand, from what we have already said, that non-being makes difficulties for the one who would refute [the statement that] it [is a being], so that whenever someone attempts the refutation, he is forced to speak of beings that are contrary to it?

THEA. What are you saying? Explain it more clearly.

PHIL. It is not to me you must look for more clarity. For when I assumed that non-being must partake of that which is neither one nor many, I spoke of
E it then, as now, as if it were one, since I speak of non-being. Do you understand?

THEA. Yes.

PHIL. And besides I also said a moment ago that it cannot be expressed in speech, be given a name, or have an account. Do you follow me?

THEA. Indeed, I follow you.

239 PHIL. Was I not speaking of contraries when I tried to join "is a being" [to a non-being]?

THEA. Clearly.

PHIL. Further, when I was joining it to a non-being, was I not treating non-being as one?

THEA. Yes.

PHIL. And again when I said it was without an account, cannot be given a name, and cannot be expressed in speech, I was therefore in my discourse making it one.

THEA. Undeniably.

PHIL. And indeed we say that if one is to speak correctly, he must define it as neither one nor many, and he must not call it "it" at all. For it would be addressed even in this discourse as one in form.

THEA. Exactly so.

B PHIL. Then what might someone say of me? For one could find that I have been defeated, both in the past and now, in my questioning of non-being. So as I said, we must not look for a correct account of non-being in what I say, but instead let us look for it in what you say.

THEA. What do you mean?

PHIL. Come now, since you are young, make a noble effort and try as best you can to avoid joining being and the one or the many in number to non-being and so say something correct about it.

C THEA. It would take a very absurd appetite for the undertaking if I should make the attempt after seeing what happened to you.

PHIL. Well, if it seems right, let us say goodbye to you and me. And until we find someone equal to the task, let us say that the sophist has very cleverly hidden in a difficult place.

THEA. Very much so, it seems.

PHIL. Hence, if we say that he possesses some sort of art of semblance, he will easily take advantage of this deficiency in discourse to twist the things
D of which we speak into their contraries. And when we call him a maker of images, he will ask us what exactly the image is of which we speak. So we must ask, Theaetetus, what will someone reply to a youth who asks this question?

THEA. It is clear that we shall say that we mean images formed in water and mirrors, and also those made by painters and sculptors, and, I suppose, all others of the same sort.

E PHIL. Plainly, Theaetetus, you have never seen a sophist.

THEA. Why?

PHIL. He will seem to you to keep his eyes shut, or to have no eyes at all.

THEA. How so?

PHIL. When you give your answer in this way to him, and you speak of something in mirrors or works of art, he will laugh at what you say when you speak to him as though he could see. He will feign ignorance of mirrors and water and even eyesight altogether, he will ask you only about the things you have said.

240 THEA. What sort of things?

PHIL. That which is common to the various things you mentioned and thought proper to call by a single name, "image," when you spoke of them all as if they were one being. So speak and defend yourself against the man and do not retreat.

THEA. What else, stranger, might we say an image is except that it is something made to be like another thing, which is real?

PHIL. Do you mean that it is "like" another thing in being real? In what way
B do you mean that it is "like" it?

THEA. [I mean that] it is not at all the real thing, but is a likeness [of the real thing].[43]

PHIL. Do you then say that the real thing really is a being?[44]

THEA. I do.

PHIL. Then is the non-real thing contrary to a real one?

THEA. Of course.

PHIL. Therefore, are you not saying that the likeness[45] really is a non-being when you say that it is a non-real thing?[46]

THEA. But it is in some way a being.

PHIL. But not in the way a real thing is a being, you mean.

THEA. Certainly not, except that it really is a likeness.

PHIL. Then, although it really is a non-being, is it not really what we call a likeness?

C THEA. There is a danger that some such compound has been made in which non-being has been intertwined with being, and it is rather absurd.

PHIL. It is absurd, is it not? You see, therefore, that the many-headed sophist has forced us, in this interchange, unwillingly to admit that in some way non-being is a being.

THEA. I see it clearly.

PHIL. Well then, how can we define his art so that we shall be able to be in agreement with ourselves?

THEA. What do you mean by this and about what sort of thing are you apprehensive?

D PHIL. When we say that he deceives us with the semblance and that his art is one of deception, shall we say that at such times our souls, under the influence of his art, hold false beliefs, or if not, what else could we say?

THEA. Just that. What else might we say?

PHIL. Again, false belief will be belief that things contrary to beings are beings, will it not?[47]

THEA. It will.

PHIL. Then you say that false belief is belief that non-beings are beings.[48]

THEA. I must say this.

E PHIL. Is it belief that non-beings are non-beings or believing that things that are *non*-beings are beings?[49]

THEA. It must be belief that things that are in some way non-beings are beings, at least if anyone is ever even in a slight degree to believe falsely.

PHIL. And is it not also belief that *beings* are *non*-beings?

THEA. Yes.

PHIL. And this too is a falsehood?

THEA. It is.

PHIL. And a statement, I suppose, will also be considered false if it states that non-beings are beings or that beings are non-beings.

241 THEA. How else could it become false?

PHIL. In virtually no other way. But a sophist will not say these things. Indeed, how is anyone of good sense to be induced to agree, when we agreed before about these things that they cannot be expressed in speech, named, given an account, or thought? Do we understand, Theaetetus, what he means?

THEA. Of course we understand that he will say that we are saying things that are contrary to those we previously said when we dared to say that there are falsehoods among beliefs and in statements. For we were often forced to
B combine being with non-being, although we agreed just now that this is not at all possible.

PHIL. Your memory is correct. But it is time for us to decide what we must do about the sophist. For if we track him down and assign to him the art of those who make falsehoods and cast spells, the objections and difficulties, you see, are many and easy to produce.

THEA. I do see this.

PHIL. We have gone through a small number of them, even though they
C are virtually more than one can count.

THEA. It would seem to be impossible to capture a sophist if this is so.

PHIL. Well, shall we back away now and give in?

THEA. I say we should not if there is in any way the slightest chance of taking hold of the man.

PHIL. So will you allow it, and in accord with what you said, be content, if we can somehow free ourselves even a little bit from so powerful an argument?

THEA. How could I not allow this?

PHIL. Then I have still another favor to ask of you.

D THEA. And what is it?

PHIL. Do not take me to be engaging in a kind of patricide.

THEA. Why should I do so?

PHIL. It will be necessary for us in order to defend ourselves to put the statement of father Parmenides to the test and to force non-being in some way to be a being, and again, to force being in some way to be a non-being.

THEA. It seems that this is the sort of thing for which we must fight in our discussion.

E PHIL. It must seem so even to a blind man, as we say. For unless these things have been rejected or accepted, one will hardly ever be able to speak about false statement or false belief, or about images, likenesses, imitations, or semblances themselves, or even about the arts, however many there are, that pertain to them, without being forced to say something that is contrary to itself and appear to be ridiculous.

THEA. Most true.

242 PHIL. For these reasons we must here and now dare to attack the statement of our father, or else we must entirely let it be if we have any hesitation that

keeps us from doing it.

THEA. Well, let nothing at all keep us from doing this.

PHIL. Then I still have a third small favor to ask of you.

THEA. You have only to mention it.

PHIL. I said just now that the refutation of this theory has always been too much for me, as in fact it still is.

THEA. So you did.

PHIL. Well, I fear that because of what has been said that I shall seem to you
to be mad when at every step I reverse my position. It is for your sake that
B we shall attempt to refute the statement [of Parmenides] if we can.

THEA. As for me, I shall not at all believe that we are doing anything improper if you should proceed to offer this refutation and demonstration. Go ahead boldly for this purpose.

PHIL. Well, how should one begin a perilous account? My boy, I think that the path we most certainly must follow is this.

THEA. What sort of path must we follow?

PHIL. First of all, we must examine things now thought to be clear so we can
be sure that we may not somehow have fallen into confusion about them and
C to be too readily agreeing with one another on the assumption that we clearly
understand them.

THEA. Tell me more clearly what you mean.

PHIL. Parmenides, and all the rest who have ever arrived at a conclusion about how many beings there are and what sort of beings there are, seem to me to have been too easily satisfied with the accounts they present to us.

THEA. How so?

PHIL. Each one seems to tell us a different story as if we were children. One
of them says that there are three beings that sometimes are at war among
themselves in various way, and at other times become friends, marry, have
children, and bring up the children. Another says that there are two beings,
D wet and dry or hot and cold, which he has live together and join in marriage.
Our own people of Elea, beginning with Xenophanes or even those before
him, tell stories in which all things, so-called, are one being. But there are
certain Ionian muses, and at a later date, Sicilian muses, determined that it
was safest to combine both stories, and to say that being is both one and
many, and is held together by enmity and friendship. The more
E intense of these muses says that it is continually separating and combining,
while the more relaxed frees it from always being this way, and says that
everything is sometimes one and friendly under the influence of Aphrodite
243 and sometimes many and at war with itself because of a kind of strife.

Regardless whether or not anyone has spoken the truth in all this, it is difficult and harsh in this way to censure the most famous men of all who have spoken of great things. But to say the following is not offensive.

THEA. To say what?

PHIL. That they have overlooked us, the many, and have shown very little concern for us. For they draw their own conclusions, each in his own way,
B without caring whether we follow what they say or are left behind.

THEA. What do you mean?

PHIL. When one of them says that beings are many, one, or two, have come to be, or are coming to be, and that hot is mixed with cold, or at some other time or place supposes that somehow there is separation and combination, do you understand, for heaven's sake, Theaetetus, what any of these things mean? For my part, when I was younger, when I heard someone speak of non-being, which is now causing difficulty, I thought I understood exactly what it is. But now you see the difficulty we have about it.

C THEA. I see it.

PHIL. Perhaps, then, we have in the soul this same state [of difficulty] about being and we claim to be without difficulty and to understand it when someone speaks of it, but about the other we do not. Yet we have [in the soul] a similar state in both cases.

THEA. Perhaps.

PHIL. And about the other things of which we have spoken[50] let the same be said.

THEA. Certainly.

PHIL. We shall examine many of these later, if you wish, but now we must examine the one that is their greatest and primary source.

D THEA. Of which of them are you speaking? Or is it obvious that you are saying that we must first investigate being in relation to what those who speak of it think is clear?

PHIL. You have understood my meaning at once, Theaetetus. I am saying that we should proceed as if they themselves were present by questioning them as follows: "Tell us, you who say that all things are hot and cold, or some such pair as this, what is it you say of both when you say that both [the hot and the cold] are being or that each is a being? How are we to understand [the cause of] this 'to be a being' of yours? Are we to suppose that for you
E there is a third thing in addition to those two [that causes them to be beings], and that everything is three beings rather than two? For surely when you call one or the other of the two things a being, you are not saying that both alike are beings. For in each case there would be one being and not two."

THEA. What you say is true.

PHIL. "But do you want to call both together a being?"

THEA. Perhaps.

244 PHIL. "But friends," we shall say, "the two would thus most clearly be said to be one being [and this is absurd]."

THEA. You are perfectly right.

PHIL. "Then since we are in difficulty [about the cause of their being], please make clear to us what it is you want to signify when you speak of a being. For it is clear that you have known these things all along, whereas we formerly thought we understood them, but now we are in difficulty. So first teach us about this in order that we may not think we understand what you say when in fact the complete contrary of this happens to be the case." If we
B say these things and deem them worthy to be said to them or to anyone else who says that all things are more than one, then my boy, we shall not be doing anything offensive, shall we?

THEA. Not at all.

PHIL. What about this? From those who say that all things are one, must we not learn as best we can what they are talking about when they speak of being?

THEA. Yes, surely.

PHIL. Then let them answer this question. "Are you saying that there is only one thing?" And they will reply, "Yes," will they not?

THEA. Yes.

PHIL. "What about this? Do you call anything a being?"

THEA. "Yes."

C PHIL. "Is it what you call one, using the two names for the same thing, or how is it?"

THEA. Stranger, what will be their answer to this question?

PHIL. Obviously, Theaetetus, he who accepts this hypothesis will not find it the easiest thing to answer this question or any other.

THEA. Why?

PHIL. It is surely ridiculous for him to agree that there are two names when he has assumed the view that there is nothing except one thing.

THEA. Certainly.

D PHIL. And it would make no sense at all for him to agree with someone who says that any name is a being.

THEA. Why?

PHIL. Because if he assumes that the name is other than the thing [named] he is, I suppose, saying that there are two beings.

THEA. Yes.

PHIL. While if he should assume that the name is the same as the thing [named], either he will be forced to speak of a name of nothing, or if he says that it is a name of anything, it will follow that the name is only the name of a name and of nothing else.

THEA. Just so.

PHIL. And, indeed, (…)[51]

THEA. Necessarily.

PHIL. Will they say that the whole is the same as or other than the one being?

E THEA. How could they deny that it is the same? They do say this.

PHIL. But if it is a whole, [it is] as Parmenides says:

> On all sides like the mass of a well-rounded sphere,
> equally poised in every direction from the middle;
> for there must be no more or less of it in any direction.

Since it is of this sort, being has a middle and extremes, and in having them, must have parts. Do you agree?

THEA. I do.

245 PHIL. But there is no reason why what has parts should not possess unity as an attribute in relation to all of its parts, and in this way be one as a whole, while being all [of its parts].

THEA. None whatever.

PHIL. But is it not impossible for what possesses unity in this way to be the one itself?

THEA. Why?

PHIL. Surely, what is really one must be said, in keeping with its correct account, to be absolutely partless.

THEA. Yes it must.

B PHIL. The sort of thing that has many parts will not agree with the account.

THEA. I understand.

PHIL. Then will being be both one and a whole because it possesses unity as an attribute, or shall we say that it is not a whole at all?

THEA. The choice you give me is a hard one.

PHIL. What you say is very true. For if being somehow possesses unity as an attribute, it will not appear to be the same as the one, and indeed, [if it is not the same,] all things will be more than one.

THEA. Yes.

C PHIL. And if being is [a whole, but] not a whole because of possessing unity as an attribute, and the whole itself is a being [of which being is said to partake], it follows that being falls short of itself.

THEA. Certainly.

PHIL. According to this account, since being is deprived of itself, it will be a non-being.

THEA. Just so.

PHIL. And so everything once again becomes more than one, since being and the whole each separately has its peculiar nature.

THEA. Yes.

PHIL. But if the whole is in its entirety a non-being, these same things belong to being, and in addition to being a non-being, it could not ever come
D to be.

THEA. Why?

PHIL. Because what has come to be always has come to be as a whole [comes to be]. So whoever denies that the whole is among beings must not call either being or what comes to be a being.

THEA. And that certainly seems to be the case.

PHIL. Moreover, the non-whole [that being is, since being cannot partake of the whole if the whole is a non-being,] cannot even be of some quantity. For if it is of some quantity, it must be a whole of whatever quantity it has.

THEA. Exactly.

PHIL. Whoever says that being is either some two things or only one will be faced with many other questions, each involving insurmountable difficulties.

E THEA. That is made clear by the difficulties now coming into view. For each is connected, one to another, leading us into a greater and more troublesome confusion about the things always said by our predecessors.

PHIL. Although we have not gone through all the views of those who give an exact account of being and non-being, nevertheless, let this suffice. We must look at those who speak of them in another way, so that we may know, from
246 all, that to say what being is is no easier than to say what non-being is.

THEA. So we must go to them.

PHIL. And indeed there seems to be something like a battle between giants and gods going on because of their argumentation about being.

THEA. Why?

PHIL. Some drag down everything from the unseen heaven to earth and really take hold of rocks and trees with their hands. For those who attach themselves to all such things of this sort affirm with conviction that only that which offers resistance and can be touched is a being. They define being as body, and when anyone says that what is without being is a being, they show
B utter contempt for him and are unwilling to listen to anything else he has to

say.

THEA. The men of whom you speak are dreadful. I myself have met many of them.

PHIL. Yes. So those who argue with them are very cautious when making a
defense from the vantage point of the unseen world above, since they force
real being to be the forms that are discerned by the mind and are without
body. The bodies their opponents claim to be reality they shatter into small
C pieces in their arguments and ascribe to them a continuous coming to be that
is contrary to being. Each side, Theaetetus, has always been fighting against
the other an endless battle over this issue.

THEA. True.

PHIL. So let us obtain from each side in turn an account of the being for whose sake they take a stand.

THEA. How shall we obtain it?

PHIL. The easier task will be to obtain one from those who suppose being to
consist in forms, since they are more civilized. To obtain an account from
those who drag down everything by force into body is not simply difficult, it
D may even be impossible. However, it seems to me that we must deal with
them in this way.

THEA. In what way?

PHIL. The best way of all, if it were somehow possible, is actually to make them better, but if that is not possible, let us make them better for the sake of the argument by assuming that they would give us a more civil answer than they are now willing to give. For an agreement from those who are better has more authority than an agreement from those who are worse. But we are not concerned about them. Rather, we seek the truth.

E THEA. Quite right.

PHIL. Tell those who have become better to answer you and you be an interpreter of their answers.

THEA. I shall.

PHIL. Let them tell us, then, whether they say that there is such a thing as a mortal animal.

THEA. Of course they do.

PHIL. Do they not agree that this is an ensouled body?

THEA. Assuredly.

PHIL. Do they include the soul among beings?

247 THEA. Yes.

PHIL. And do they not say that one soul is just and another unjust, one wise and another foolish?

THEA. Of course.

PHIL. And do they not say that each soul becomes just by the possession and presence of justice, and contrary by the possession of the contrary?

THEA. They make that admission too.

PHIL. But surely they will say that what can come to be present or absent in a thing is in every way a being.

THEA. Indeed, they say this.

B PHIL. If justice and wisdom and any other virtue and their contraries, and also the soul in which these become present, are beings, do they say that any of them are visible and tangible, or that all are invisible?

THEA. That virtually none of them is visible.

PHIL. What about these things? Do they say that any of them have some sort of body?

THEA. To that question as a whole they no longer have a single answer. It seems to them that the soul herself has some sort of body, but as for wisdom and each of the other things about which you asked, they are ashamed boldly to agree that none are beings or to affirm that all are bodies.

C PHIL. Clearly, Theaetetus, they have become better men for our sake, since those born of the earth from dragon's teeth[52] would not be ashamed to speak in one of these ways and would insist that anything they cannot squeeze with their hands is nothing at all.

THEA. You express their thought fairly closely.

PHIL. Then let us question them again. For if they are willing to admit that
among beings there is even a small one that is without body, that is sufficient.
D They must say what it is that has become common to these and to those with
body and that they have in view when they say that both are beings. Perhaps
they would at once be in difficulty, and if they were in such straits, consider
whether they would be willing to entertain and agree to a proposal about
being we might make.

THEA. What sort of proposal? Tell me and we shall soon find out.

PHIL. I say that whatever has any power, either to act upon another thing or
to be affected even in the smallest degree by the most insignificant
E thing, even if only once, is a being in the perfect way being is. For I propose
as a definition to define beings that they are nothing but power.

THEA. Since they do not have for the moment anything better to say, they accept this.

PHIL. Very good. Perhaps later it may seem otherwise both to them and to us. However, for the present, let us remain in agreement about this.

248 THEA. We shall.

PHIL. Let us turn to the others, the friends of the forms, and once more you shall be for us an interpreter of their answers.

THEA. I shall.

PHIL. "You make a distinction, I suppose, in which what comes to be and being are separate, do you not?"

THEA. "We do."

PHIL. "And you say that we commune with what comes to be by means of sensation in the body and with real being by means of reasoning in the soul, and that being always remains the same, while what comes to be is different at different times."

B THEA. "That is what we say."

PHIL. "But, most excellent men, what are we to say that you mean when you speak of communion in both cases? Is it not what we were just now talking about?"

THEA. "What is that?"

PHIL. "It is an acting upon something or a being affected by something that comes to be because of some power exhibited by things that meet with one another." You will not hear their response to this, but perhaps I hear it because of my contact with them.

THEA. What account do they give of it?

C PHIL. They do not agree with the statement about being we just made to those born of the earth.

THEA. Which of our statements?

PHIL. We assumed a sufficient definition of beings to be the presence of a power to act upon something or to be affected by something in even the smallest degree.

THEA. Yes.

PHIL. In reply they say that what comes to be partakes of the power to act upon something or to be affected by something, but neither power is compatible with being.

THEA. Is there not something to this reply?

PHIL. Yes, but in response to this we must tell them that we need to know more clearly whether they agree that the soul knows, and that being is known.

D THEA. They certainly agree.

PHIL. "Then do you say that knowing or being known is an acting upon something or a being affected by something or both? Or that the one is a being affected by something and the other an acting upon something else? Or that neither partakes of either of the two?"

THEA. Clearly they would say that neither partakes of either an acting upon something or a being affected by something, since otherwise they would be saying things contrary to those they said before.

PHIL. I see. That is, if knowing is acting upon something, it must follow that what is known is affected by something. Since if being, on this theory, is known by knowing it, just insofar as it is being known it is in motion because
E it is being affected, which we say would not happen to what is at rest.

THEA. Quite right.

PHIL. By Zeus, are we to be so easily persuaded that in reality motion, life, soul, and thought are not present in the perfect being, and that a being in this state neither lives nor thinks but is awesome and holy, without mind, and is without motion?

249 THEA. That would be a terrible thing to say, stranger.

PHIL. Well, then, may we say that it has mind but not life?

THEA. How is that possible?

PHIL. But in saying that both are present in the perfect being, can we deny that it has them in soul?

THEA. In what other way could it have them?

PHIL. But can it possess mind, life, and soul, and yet insofar as it is ensouled, remain entirely without motion?

B THEA. All of these things seem to me to be unreasonable.

PHIL. And both what is in motion and motion [itself] must be admitted to be beings.

THEA. Undeniably.

PHIL. It follows then, Theaetetus, that if beings are not in motion, nowhere is mind present in anything or concerned with anything.

THEA. Exactly.

PHIL. Yet if we should agree that all things are coming to be and are in motion, by this account also we would exclude from beings this same thing.[53]

THEA. How?

C PHIL. Does it seem to you that, without rest, things would ever come to be the same in number, quality, or relation?

THEA. Not at all.

PHIL. And without these things can you see how mind could be a being or come to be anywhere?

THEA. I cannot.

PHIL. And so we must fight with every argument against him who would make strong claims about anything whatsoever while doing away with knowledge, thought, and mind.

THEA. Certainly.

PHIL. So for these reasons it seems that a philosopher who values these
things above all others must not accept the theory that all things are at rest,
either from those who maintain that there is one form or from those who
D maintain that there are many; nor again must he at all listen to those who
have being be in motion in every way. But like children who request [both
when offered a choice of two things], he must say that being and all things
are both [at rest and in motion].

THEA. Most true.

PHIL. So we seem to have gotten a fairly good hold of being with our account, have we not?

THEA. Yes.

PHIL. Wait a minute! It seems to me, Theaetetus, that we are now on the verge of knowing how difficult our search is.

E THEA. Once more, what do you mean by this?

PHIL. My dear young man, do you not see that we are now most ignorant about it in spite of seeming to ourselves to be saying something?

THEA. That is certainly true of me, but I do not understand very well how we again have failed to notice that we were in such a state.

PHIL. Then let us consider very carefully whether we, in agreeing now to these things, could be rightly asked the very questions we ourselves put to those who say that all things are hot and cold.

250 THEA. What questions? Remind me.

PHIL. Very well. I shall try to do so by questioning you exactly as I then questioned them, so that we may go forward at the same time.

THEA. Very good.

PHIL. Very well then. Do you not say that motion and rest are most contrary to one another?

THEA. They are so.

PHIL. And yet you say that both and each of them equally are beings?

B THEA. I do.

PHIL. When you agree that they are beings, are you saying that both and each are in motion?

THEA. Not at all.

PHIL. But when you say that both are beings, are you indicating that they are at rest?

THEA. Certainly not.

PHIL. Then were you supposing that being is a third thing in the soul, in addition to these, on the ground that both motion and rest are embraced by it, and did you comprehend and look at them in their combination with being, and for this reason say that both are beings?

C THEA. We dare to divine being as a real third thing when we say that motion and rest are beings.

PHIL. Therefore, being is not motion and rest both at once, but something other than them.

THEA. So it seems.

PHIL. Therefore, being, according to its own nature, is neither in motion nor at rest.

THEA. It is so.

PHIL. Where indeed is one to direct his thought if he wants to establish for himself something clear about it?

THEA. Where indeed?

PHIL. I think it is no longer easy to direct one's thought in any direction. For
D if not in motion, how can it not be at rest? Or if it is in no way at rest how can it not be in motion? And now being has emerged outside of both of them. Is this possible?[54]

THEA. It is indeed an utter impossibility.

PHIL. However, there is something else we ought to remember.

THEA. And what is that?

PHIL. When we asked to what we must apply the name of non-being, we ran into all sorts of difficulties. Do you remember?

THEA. I do.

E PHIL. And surely we are in no less difficulty now concerning being, are we?

THEA. It seems to me, stranger, that we are in greater difficulty, if that is possible.

PHIL. Then let this be our statement of the difficulty. But since being and non-being are equally difficult for us, there is now already the hope that as one of these becomes clearer or more obscure, so will the other. And again,
251 if we should not be able to see either of them, we shall at least push our account between both at once as creditably as we can.

THEA. Good.

PHIL. Then let us explain how it is on any given occasion that we call the same thing by many names.

THEA. Like what? Give an example.

PHIL. We speak of a human being, for instance, and call him by many other names, bringing to him colors, shapes, sizes, vices, and virtues. In all of these cases and in countless others, we call him not only a human being, but also
B good and an indefinite number of other things. And for this same reason we speak of all other things in this way: while supposing that each thing is one,

we say it is many and call it by many names.

THEA. True.

PHIL. And it is for this reason, I think, that we have provided a feast for the
young and the late learners among the old. For it is easy for all to object
immediately that many things cannot be one and that one thing cannot be
many. And indeed, I suppose, they are happy to forbid us to call a man good,
but to allow us only to call the good good or the man man. For, Theaetetus,
C you often come across those who take such things seriously; sometimes they
are older men who, from poverty of thought, marvel at such things and think
that they have found in this some considerable wisdom.

THEA. Indeed, I have come across them.

PHIL. So that our account may pertain to all who have ever said anything
about being, let the questions we are about to ask be directed to these and to
D the others with whom we conversed before.

THEA. What are these questions?

PHIL. Should we refuse to attach being to motion and rest, or anything to anything else, and suppose in our discourse that beings do not blend and cannot partake of one another? Or should we unite all beings into [one and] the same [being] because they can combine with one another? Or should we say that some can combine with others and others cannot? Which of these, Theaetetus, shall we say that they would choose?

E THEA. I have no answer to give on their behalf.

PHIL. Then why not answer each of the questions one at a time and consider the consequences that ensue in each case?

THEA. Very good.

PHIL. So let us suppose, if you like, that they first say that nothing has any power to combine with anything else. Thus, neither motion nor rest can participate at all in being?

252 THEA. No.

PHIL. Then will either of them be a being if it does not combine with being?

THEA. Neither will.

PHIL. By this admission, it seems, every theory is at once uprooted, the theory of those who make all things be in motion, the theory of those who make all stand still as one thing, and the theory of those who say that beings are always in the same condition and always in the same way in accordance with their forms. For all of these attach "is a being" to things, some saying that they really are in motion, and others saying that they really stand still.

THEA. Exactly.

B PHIL. Then again, there are those who at one time combine all things and at another time separate them, regardless whether they combine them into one thing or separate them out of one thing, or whether the elements are indefinite or definite in number, and likewise, whether they suppose that this occurs alternately or always. In saying all these things, they would be saying nothing if there is no blending.

THEA. Quite true.

PHIL. The most ridiculous thing of all would be for us to adopt the theory of those who do not allow us to call one thing by the name of another because they share a common quality.

C THEA. Why?

PHIL. Because they must, I suppose, always use "is a being," as well as "separately," "from others," and "in itself," and many more besides. Since they are powerless to keep away from them or to avoid attaching them [to other words] in their statements, they do not need others to question their theory. The enemy who will oppose them, as the saying goes, is in their own household, and they go about carrying within themselves its hidden voice that is like that of the amazing Eurycles.[55]

D THEA. Your comparison to Eurycles is truly apt.

PHIL. But next, should we allow all things to have the power to combine with one another?

THEA. Even I can dispose of this.

PHIL. How?

THEA. Motion itself would completely be at rest, and rest, in turn, would be in motion, if they could supervene on one another.[56]

PHIL. But of course, it is utterly impossible that motion be at rest or that rest be in motion.

THEA. To be sure.

PHIL. Only the third alternative remains.

THEA. Yes.

E PHIL. Certainly one of the three alternatives must be true; either all will blend, none will, or some will and others will not.

THEA. Of course.

PHIL. And the first two were found to be impossible.

THEA. Yes.

PHIL. Therefore, whoever wants to answer our question correctly will adopt the third alternative.

THEA. Exactly.

253 PHIL. Then, as some things will do this, and others will not, they would be affected very much as letters of the alphabet are. For some of them, I

suppose, do not join with one another and others do.
THEA. Of course.
PHIL. And the vowels are different from the others in being like a bond that holds all together so that without one of them the others cannot be joined to one another.
THEA. Quite so.
PHIL. Now does everyone know which sort can combine with which sort, or must he who is to do this properly need an art?
THEA. He needs an art.
PHIL. Which art?
THEA. Grammar.
B PHIL. Again is not this true of high and low sounds? He who has the art to recognize which mix and which do not, is learned in music, while he who does not understand this is not.
THEA. Just so.
PHIL. And we shall find similar things to be true even in the other arts and in what lacks art.
THEA. To be sure.
PHIL. Because we have also agreed that kinds, in the same way, blend with one another, isn't it necessary for whomever journeys through our discourse have some knowledge if he intends to demonstrate correctly what sorts of kinds agree with what sorts, and what sorts do not receive one another? Is this knowledge not especially necessary if he is to show whether there are
C some that hold all together so that they can blend, and again, where there are separations, whether there are other causes of the separation of wholes?
THEA. He will certainly need knowledge and perhaps the greatest.
PHIL. Well, now, Theaetetus, what shall we call this knowledge? Or, by Zeus, have we unwittingly stumbled upon the knowledge of those who are free? Are we about to find the philosopher first, although we have been seeking a sophist?
THEA. What are you saying?
D PHIL. To separate things by kinds, not to believe that the same form is another or that another is the same, shall we not say that this is dialectical knowledge?
THEA. Yes, we shall certainly say this.
PHIL. Then he who can do this properly discerns one idea everywhere extended through many [forms], each of which remains apart, and many ideas, which are other than one another and embraced from without by one,
E and again, he discerns one idea connected in a unity through many wholes,

and many ideas entirely marked off apart. This is to know by kind how to distinguish in what way each [form] can or cannot be combined.
THEA. Absolutely.
PHIL. And I think you will assign the art of dialectic to no one else except to a pure and rightful lover of wisdom.
THEA. How could anyone assign it to anyone else?
PHIL. Then both now and in the future we shall find the philosopher in some such place as this if we should search for him; and it is also difficult to see him clearly, though the difficulty is of a different character than the difficulty
254 of seeing the sophist.
THEA. How is it different?
PHIL. The sophist, who retreats into the darkness of non-being and with practice lays hold of it, is difficult to observe because of the darkness of the place. Do you agree?
THEA. It seems likely.
PHIL. But the philosopher, who remains, through reasoning, always close to the idea of being, is not at all easy to see because of the brightness of the place; for the eyes of the soul of the many cannot bear the vision of the divine.
B THEA. This is no less likely to be true than what you said of the sophist.
PHIL. So we shall examine this matter more closely later if we should still desire to do so. But as for the sophist, I suppose, it is clear that we must not let up until we have a good look at him.
THEA. Well said.
PHIL. We agree, therefore, that some of the kinds will combine with one another and that others will not, some combining with few and others with many, and that nothing prevents those that pervade all from being combined
C with all. Next, so that we may not be bothered with many forms, let us not follow up with a discussion of all of the forms, but take only those that are called the greatest. First of all, let us consider what they are, and then how they are able to combine with one another. For if in this way we cannot grasp being and non-being perfectly clearly, we shall at least not lack an account of them insofar as the method of inquiry now followed allows. So let us in this way see whether we are allowed to say that non-being really is a non-being, and escape unharmed.
D THEA. Yes, this is what we have to do.
PHIL. Now the greatest kinds are those we have just been considering, being itself, rest, and motion.
THEA. Yes, of course.

PHIL. However, we say that the two last cannot be blended.

THEA. Indeed, they cannot.

PHIL. But being blends with both, since, in fact, both are beings.

THEA. Of course.

PHIL. Then they come to be three.

THEA. To be sure.

PHIL. So each of these three is other than the other two and the same as itself.

E THEA. Yes.

PHIL. What have we said just now in speaking of the same and the other? Are they two kinds, different from the former three, though necessarily always blended with them, so that we must investigate five beings rather than three? Or are we unwittingly speaking of one of them when we call them by the names of the same and the other?

255 THEA. Perhaps.

PHIL. But surely motion and rest are neither [the] other nor the same.

THEA. Why not?

PHIL. Whatever we should say of motion and rest in common cannot be either of them.

THEA. Why not?

PHIL. Because motion will be at rest, and rest in turn, will be in motion. For in both cases, whichever of the two comes to be the other will force the other, in turn, to change to the contrary of its own nature insofar as it partakes of
B the contrary.

THEA. Just so.

PHIL. Now both of them partake of the same and the other.

THEA. Yes.

PHIL. Thus we should not say that motion or rest is the same or the other.

THEA. We should not.

PHIL. Then must we think of being and the same as one thing?

THEA. Perhaps.

PHIL. But if being and the same do not signify different things, then when we say that both motion and rest are beings, we shall thereby be speaking of both of them as the same.

C THEA. But that is surely impossible.

PHIL. Therefore, it is impossible that the same and being are one thing.

THEA. This is more or less true.

PHIL. Then let us suppose that the same is a fourth form, in addition to the three.

THEA. Certainly.

PHIL. Now should we say that the other is a fifth? Or must we conceive of "the other" and "being" as a pair of names for one kind?

THEA. It could be.

PHIL. Still, I think that you agree that some beings are spoken of by themselves and others are always spoken of in relation to others.

THEA. Of course.

D PHIL. And the other is always spoken of in relation to something else, is it not?

THEA. Yes.

PHIL. But this would not be so if being and the other were not very different. But if the other partook of both forms [of being spoken of], as being does, there would sometimes also be among the others what is other not in relation to something else. In fact, for us, whatever should be other, as a necessary consequence, is just what is other than something else.

THEA. It is just as you say.

E PHIL. Then we must say that among the forms we have chosen to discuss, the nature of the other is a fifth.[57]

THEA. Yes.

PHIL. And we shall say that it pervades all [of the others]. For each one is other than the others not because of its own nature, but because it partakes of the idea of the other.[58]

THT. Exactly.

PHIL. Thus let us speak of the five kinds by taking them up one at a time.

THT. How?

PHIL. First of all, we say that motion is completely other than rest, do we not?

THT. We do.

PHIL. Therefore, motion is a non-rest.[59]

THT. [It is in fact] a *non*-[rest].[60]

256 PHIL. Yet it is a being since it partakes of being.

THT. It is a being.

PHIL. Again, motion is other than the same.

THT. So it seems.

PHIL. Therefore, it is a non-the same.

THT. It certainly is a non-[the same].

PHIL. Yet again, motion, as we saw, is the same, since everything [other than the same] partakes of the same.

THT. Certainly.

PHIL. Then we must agree without dissent that indeed motion is both the same and a non-the same. For when we say this, we have not spoken of the

same and non-the same in the same way. For we say that it is the same because it partakes of the same in relation to itself, and that it is a non-the
B same because of its combination with the other, because of which, since it is separate from the same, it does not become that but other, with the consequence that it is also correct to say that it is a non-the same.

THT. By all means.

PHIL. Thus if motion itself were somehow participating in rest, there would be no absurdity in saying that it is at rest.

THT. Perfectly true, if we are to admit that some of the kinds will blend with one another and others will not.

C PHIL. Indeed, we arrived at a demonstration of this [blending] in the earlier discussion in which we showed by questioning that such is their nature.

THT. Why deny it?

PHIL. Then, let us repeat ourselves. Motion is other than the other, just as it was other than the same and rest.

THT. Necessarily.

PHIL. Therefore, according to the present account, it is somehow both an other and a non-other.

THT. True.

PHIL. Then what is our next step? Shall we say that it is other than the other three, but not that it is other than the fourth, although we agreed[61] that there were five to be examined by us?

D THT. How can that be, since it is not possible to admit a smaller number than what is evident now?

PHIL. Therefore, should we have no fears in contending that motion is other than being?

THT. No fears whatsoever.

PHIL. Then it is clear that motion really is a non-being, and that it is a being because it partakes of being?

THT. Absolutely clear.

PHIL. Therefore, non-being must be a being in relation both to motion[62] and to all the kinds [other than being].[63] For in relation to all of the [other] kinds, the nature of the other renders each one a non-being[64] by making it other than
E a being, and so, in the same way, we may correctly say of all of them that they are non-beings, and again, that they are also beings because they partake of being.

THT. That seems to be true.

PHIL. In relation to each of the forms [other than being], therefore, being is many in number and non-being is unlimited in number.[65]

THT. It seems so.

257 PHIL. Then also being itself, we should say, is other than the others.

THT. It must be.

PHIL. Therefore, for us, being is a non-being inasmuch as the others are beings. For while it is not these, it is itself one thing, and again, it is not the others, which are unlimited in number.

THEA. That is just about right.

PHIL. Then we must not be displeased by these things, since it is the nature of the kinds to combine with one another. And if anyone does not admit these things, he must overcome our previous arguments before he should attempt to overcome what follows from them.

THEA. Most correctly said.

B PHIL. And now let us look at this.

THEA. What?

PHIL. When we speak of a non-being, it seems, we do not speak of something contrary to a being, but only of something that is other than it.

THEA. How so?

PHIL. For example, when we say that something is non-large, do we ever seem to you to reveal by the word the small, any more than the equal in relation to size?[66]

THEA. Of course not.

PHIL. Therefore, when it is said that the negative signifies a contrary, we shall not admit that, but only that the prefix "non-" reveals something that is
C other in relation to the words that follow it, or rather, that it reveals something that is other with respect to the things to which the names uttered after the negative are assigned.

THEA. Certainly.

PHIL. Let us think about the following, if it seems good to you.

THEA. What?

PHIL. It seems to me that the nature of the other is divided into parts, just as knowledge is.[67]

THEA. How so?

PHIL. Knowledge, I suppose, is one thing, and yet each part of it that is concerned with a particular subject and is distinguished has a name of its very own. This is why we speak of many arts and forms of knowledge.

D THEA. By all means.

PHIL. The same is true of the parts of the single nature of the other.[68]

THEA. Perhaps, but how should we speak of it?

PHIL. Is there a part of the other that is a contrast to the beautiful?[69]

THEA. There is.

PHIL. And do we say that it is nameless, or that it has a name?

THEA. It has a name. For what in each case we call non-beautiful is what is other than nothing other than the nature of the beautiful.[70]

PHIL. Tell me about this.

E THEA. About what?

PHIL. Does it follow from this that the non-beautiful is a being of some one kind marked off [from others], and again, a contrast to some another being?

THEA. It does.

PHIL. It follows, it seems, that the non-beautiful is some sort of contrast of a being to a being.

THEA. Perfectly true.

PHIL. Then according to this account, do we think that the beautiful is more of a being, while the non-beautiful is less?

THEA. Not at all.

258 PHIL. So must we speak of the large and the non-large in the same way?

THEA. We must.

PHIL. Then should we also suppose that we must speak of the just and the non-just in the same way, in that neither is more a being than the other?

THEA. Obviously.

PHIL. And we shall speak of the others in the same way. Since the nature of the other has been shown to be a being, and since it is a being, it is necessary, indeed, to suppose that its parts also are beings in no less degree.

THEA. Of course.

B PHIL. Then it seems that the contrast in which a part of the nature of the other and the nature of being are set against one another[71] is, if we may speak in this way, a being no less than is being itself [to whose nature the part of the nature of the other is set in contrast], since the contrast does not signify what is contrary to being, but only what is other in relation to it.

THEA. That is very clear.

PHIL. Then what shall we call it?

THEA. It is evident that it is the very non-being for which we were searching because of the sophist.

PHIL. So, as you said, is it less of a being than any of the others? Should one now have the courage to say that non-being assuredly is a being and has a nature of its own, and that just as the large was [called] large, the beautiful beautiful, the non-large non-large and the non-beautiful non-beautiful, so in
C the same way non-being was and is [said to be] a non-being, to be counted as one form among many beings? Or do we have doubt about this, Theaetetus?

THEA. None at all.

PHIL. Then do you realize that we have doubted the testimony of Parmenides and gone far beyond the limits of his prohibition.

THEA. How have we done this?

PHIL. We have not only pursued an inquiry he did not allow, but by searching further we have presented him with a demonstration.

THEA. How?

D PHIL. Because somewhere he says:

> Never let it prevail that non-beings are beings.
> In pursuit of the truth, keep your thought from this path.

THEA. That is what he says.

PHIL. We have not only demonstrated that non-beings are beings, but have even brought to light the form that is in fact non-being. For we have demonstrated that the nature of the other is a being and is parceled out over
E all [other] beings in relation to one another, and we dared to say of the part of its nature that is a contrast to being in relation to each thing,[72] that this itself *is* non-being.

THEA. We seem to have arrived at a statement, Stranger, which to my mind is perfectly true.

PHIL. Let no one say to us that we are showing non-being to be contrary to being when we dare to say that it is a being. For we long ago said goodbye to any contrary to being, whether it is or is not a being and has an account or
259 has no account at all. In relation to what we have said non-being to be, let someone either question us and persuade us that we do not speak well, or so long as he cannot do that, he must say what we say: (i) that the kinds blend with one another, (ii) that being and the other pervade all [others] and one another, (iii) that the other, by partaking of being is a being because of this partaking, yet is not that of which it partakes, but other, (iv) that since it is other than being, it necessarily and most clearly is a non-being, (v) that being, in turn, which participates in the other, would be other than the other kinds, (vi) that since it is other than all those, it is not each of those, it is not each of
B them or all the others, but itself, and so (vii) it cannot be denied that being, in relation to thousands upon thousands of things, is a non-being, and the others, both in individually and collectively, are beings in many ways and non-beings in many ways.

THEA. True.

PHIL. If someone has doubts about these [apparent] contrarieties, he must conduct his own investigation and say something better than what has been

said now. But if he thinks he has come up with something difficult, and
enjoys dragging words sometimes to one thing and at other times to another,
C he has made serious an endeavor not worthy of much serious attention, as
our present discussions show. For to discover this is neither clever nor
difficult; what is both difficult and beautiful is to discover something else.

THEA. What is that?

PHIL. What has been said before: to let go of these endless quibbles and to
be able to follow each of the things said when someone should say that in
some way another being is the same or that the same being is another, and
question in each case the way in which, and in relation to what, he says one
or the other has been affected. To show that in some way the same is other
D or that the other is the same, that the large is small, or that the like is unlike,
and so to enjoy always bringing forward contraries in discussions, is not true
refutation and is clearly the offspring of someone who has just come into
contact with beings.

THEA. Assuredly.

PHIL. My good lad, the attempt to separate everything from everything else
is the discordant act of someone who is entirely lacking in learning and
philosophy.

E THEA. Why?

PHIL. This separation of each thing from everything else completely
destroys all discourse, since discourse has come about for us because of the
weaving together of the forms with one another.

THEA. True.

260 PHIL. Notice then that we fought our battle with those persons [who would
destroy discourse] at the right time and forced them to allow the blending of
one form with another.

THEA. Why was it fought?

PHIL. Because discourse for us is one of the kinds of beings. The most im-
portant point is that, if we were deprived of this, we would be deprived of
philosophy. Our present situation requires us to agree about what discourse is,
and if its very being were taken away from us, I suppose that we would not
be able to speak at all. We would have been deprived of it if we had agreed
B that there is no blending of anything with anything.

THEA. This much is true, but I do not understand why we must agree now
about discourse.

PHIL. Perhaps you might understand more easily if you follow in this way.

THEA. In what way?

PHIL. Non-being appeared to us to be one being, a certain kind among others, and to be sown in every being.

THEA. It did.

PHIL. So the next thing is to inquire whether it blends with what is believed and said.[73]

THEA. Why?

PHIL. If non-being does not blend with them, all [that is believed and said]
C must be true; but if it does blend with them, belief and discourse become false. For to believe that non-beings are beings and to speak of non-beings as beings, I suppose, is for falsehood to come to be in thought and discourse.

THEA. It is so.

PHIL. And if a falsehood is a being, deception is a being.

THEA. Yes.

PHIL. And if deception is a being, then all things must be filled with both images and likenesses, and with semblance.

THEA. Of course.

D PHIL. But we said that the sophist fled somewhere into this place and that he totally denied that a falsehood is a being because non-being cannot be expressed either in thought or in discourse, non-being not in any way participating in being.

THEA. Yes, this is what was said.

PHIL. Since it has been shown that non-being partakes of being, perhaps he would no longer fight the battle in this way. He might, however, say that some forms partake of non-being, others do not, and that what is said and believed are among those that do not. Thus he might once more fight the battle over the arts of image-making and semblance-making that we say he
E possesses, [this time] on the ground that they are non-beings, since what is believed and said do not combine with non-being. For a falsehood is at all a being unless this combination occurs. Therefore we must first examine what discourse, belief, and perceptual judgment are so that when they come into view we may observe the combination with non-being, and upon observing this, we may demonstrate that falsehood is a being, and having demonstrated
261 that, we may imprison the sophist in this kind, if he is liable, or if we release him, look for him in another kind.

THEA. Indeed, stranger, it seems that what you said at the beginning about the sophist, that his kind would be difficult to catch, was true. For he seems to have many defenses, and when he sets one up, first we must fight a battle
B against it before we reach him himself, since now that we have with great difficulty crossed over the defense that non-being is not a being, he has set up another defense, and we must now demonstrate that there is falsehood in

discourse and belief, and after this, perhaps, there will be another defense and yet another after that, and it seems there will be no limit to them.

PHIL. One must take courage, Theaetetus, if he is to always be able to make even a little progress. For what would one who is discouraged about these matters do about others if he accomplishes nothing in relation to them or
C even suffers a setback? As the proverb says, hardly at all could someone of this sort capture the city. But now, my good lad, since the defense about which you spoke has been crossed over, the largest wall has been taken and the others now are smaller and easier to take.

THEA. Well said.

PHIL. Let me first take discourse and belief, as I said just now, so that we may provide a clearer account of whether non-being has contact with them or whether both are entirely true and neither is ever false.

THEA. Very good.

D PHIL. Then let us investigate names in just the same way we did the forms and letters about which we spoke. For what we seek now comes into sight in the same way.

THEA. And what shall we ask about names?

PHIL. Whether all fit together with one another, or none, or whether some will and others will not.

THEA. It is clear, of course, that some will and others will not.

PHIL. Perhaps what you mean is that there are some things that are said in succession and that reveal something fit together, while others that are said in
E sequence and signify nothing do not.

THEA. But what do you mean?

PHIL. That to which I thought you agreed when you answered. For we have, it seems, two kinds of things in spoken sound that reveal something about substantial being.

THEA. What are they?

262 PHIL. One is called names and the other is called verbs.

THEA. Explain each.

PHIL. The one that reveals something in relation to actions, I suppose, we call a verb.

THEA. Yes.

PHIL. The one that is a vocal sign applied to those who perform these actions we call a name.

THEA. Exactly.

PHIL. Therefore, discourse is not ever comprised of names alone spoken in succession, or again, of verbs spoken without names.

THEA. I do not understand these words.

B PHIL. Then it is clear that you were looking to something else just now when you agreed. For the very thing I wanted to say was that things said in succession in this way are not discourse.

THEA. In what way?

PHIL. For instance, when someone says "walks," "runs," or "sleeps," and many other verbs that signify actions, even if said one after another, he does not, for all that, create discourse.

THEA. Of course not.

PHIL. And again, when in succession "lion," "stag," "horse" and however many other names of those who perform actions are uttered, no discourse yet comes about. In neither case do the spoken sounds reveal an action or an
C inaction, or the being of a being or of a non-being, until someone should mix verbs with names. Then the words fit together and the first combination immediately becomes discourse of the primary and shortest kind.

THEA. What do you mean?

PHIL. When someone says, "Man learns," would you say that this is primary discourse in its briefest form?

D THEA. Certainly.

PHIL. For it reveals something, I suppose, about things that are, are coming to be, have come to be, or will be, and not only names something, but brings something about by weaving verbs together with names. That is why we said that it does not only name something, but also that it says something, and why we use the name, "discourse," for the interweaving.

THEA. True.

PHIL. And thus just as some things do and others do not fit together, also, again, some vocal signs do and others do not fit together, and those that fit together comprise discourse.

E THEA. Exactly.

PHIL. Furthermore, here is one small point.

THEA. What is it?

PHIL. Whenever there is discourse, it must be about something; it cannot not be about something.

THEA. Just so.

PHIL. And must it not also be of a certain sort?

THEA. Of course.

PHIL. Now let us direct our attention to ourselves.

THEA. Let it be so.

PHIL. Then I shall say something to you in which I shall combine a thing with an action by means of [combining] a name and a verb, and you tell me what it is about which I am speaking.

263 THEA. I shall do my best.

PHIL. "Theaetetus sits." It is not a long piece of discourse, is it?

THEA. No, but sufficient.

PHIL. Now it is your job to tell me what it concerns and is about.

THEA. It is clear that it concerns me and is about me.

PHIL. And again, what about this?

THEA. What?

PHIL. "Theaetetus," to whom I am now speaking, "flies."

THEA. This too, one would say, is about no one else but me and concerns me.

PHIL. And we said that each of the pieces of discourse must be of a certain sort.

B THEA. Yes.

PHIL. And of what sort must we say each is?

THEA. The one, I suppose, is false and the other true.

PHIL. Among these the true one reports beings concerning you as beings.[74]

THEA. To be sure.

PHIL. The false one [reports] other beings [as beings concerning you].

THEA. Yes.

PHIL. Therefore, it reports non-beings as beings [concerning you].

THEA. It would appear so.

PHIL. [It reports] other beings concerning you, since we said, I believe, that there are many beings and many non-beings in relation to each thing.

THEA. Exactly.

C PHIL. Now concerning the last piece of discourse I uttered about you, it must, first of all, be one of the shortest pieces according to our definition of what discourse is.

THEA. Now, at least, we agreed to that.

PHIL. Secondly, it is a piece of discourse about something.

THEA. It is.

PHIL. And if it is not about you, it is not about anything else.

THEA. Certainly not.

PHIL. But if it were about nothing, it would not be discourse at all. For we showed that discourse about nothing cannot possibly be discourse.

THEA. Most true.

D PHIL. Indeed when things are said concerning you, but things other as the same, or non-beings as beings, it by all means seems that a combination of this sort that comes to be from verbs and names is in reality false discourse.

THEA. Absolutely true.

PHIL. And what now? Is it not already clear that these kinds — thought, belief, and perceptual judgment, all arise in our souls as things false and true?

THEA. How is it clear?

PHIL. You will see more easily if you first grasp [an account of] what they are and how each differs from the others.

THEA. Just give me [the account].

E PHIL. Thought and discourse, then, are the same, except that what we call thought is the conversation the soul has with itself without spoken sound.

THEA. Certainly.

PHIL. While the stream that flows from the soul through the mouth with sound has been called discourse.

THEA. True.

PHIL. And in discourse, we know there is...

THEA. There is what?

PHIL. Affirmation and denial.

THEA. We know this.

264 PHIL. Now when this happens within the soul in relation to silent thought, do you have anything to call it except belief?

THEA. How could I?

PHIL. And when belief is present in the soul not by itself, but because of sensation, then can a condition of this sort, again, be correctly called anything else than appearing to be?

THEA. It cannot.

PHIL. So there is true and false discourse, and of the kinds of things under consideration, thought was seen to be a conversation of the soul with itself, belief was seen to be a conclusion of thought, and what we say appears to be
B is a blending of sensation and belief. Consequently, since these and discourse are of the same kind, on some occasions some must be false.

THEA. Certainly.

PHIL. So do you understand that we have discovered what false belief and false discourse are sooner than we anticipated when we a little while ago feared that in seeking this we might be taking on an endless task?

THEA. I understand.

C PHIL. Then let us not be without the courage to complete our undertaking. For now that these matters have become clear, let us recall the divisions we made earlier according to forms.

THEA. Which divisions?

PHIL. We distinguished two forms of the art of image-making, the arts of likeness-making and semblance-making.

THEA. Yes.

PHIL. We said we were perplexed about where we would put a sophist.

THEA. We did.

PHIL. And while we were perplexed about this, we were plunged into a still greater swirl of darkness when the argument appeared that challenged everything [we said], arguing that neither a likeness, nor an image, nor a semblance is a being at all, since falsehood is never a being.

D THEA. True.

PHIL. But now since false discourse and false belief have been shown to be beings, imitations of beings can be beings and because of this state of affairs an art of deception can come to be.

THEA. They can.

PHIL. And we agreed earlier that [the art of] a sophist belongs to one or the other of these [forms of the art of image-making].

THEA. Yes.

PHIL. Then let us try again, after splitting the proposed kind into two, to proceed along the right-hand part of that which has been divided, holding on
E to the association of the sophist [with that part], until we have stripped away all things he has in common [with others] and when we are left with his peculiar nature, let us show it primarily to ourselves, but also to those
265 who have a natural kinship with such a method.

THEA. Right.

PHIL. So we began by distinguishing the productive art from the acquisitive?

THEA. Yes.

PHIL. He was seen by us in some such forms of acquisition as hunting, competition, and commerce?

THEA. Certainly.

PHIL. But now since the art of imitation has embraced him, it is clear that we must first divide the productive art into two. For we say, I suppose, that
B imitation is a sort of production of images rather than of the things of which they are images. Do you agree?

THEA. Absolutely.

PHIL. Then let there be two parts of the productive art.

THEA. What are they?

PHIL. The divine and the human.

THEA. I do not yet understand.

PHIL. Let us recall what was said at the beginning. We said that the art of producing things has the power that could cause things that previously were non-beings to come to be at a later time.

THEA. I remember.

C PHIL. Consider all mortal creatures, all the animals and all the plants that grow on the earth from seeds or roots, and all lifeless bodies formed in the earth, whether fusible or not. Shall we not say that they were previously non-beings and later came to be beings by the craftsmanship of God and no one else? Or shall we accept what the many believe and say?

THEA. What is that?

PHIL. [Shall we say] that nature gives birth to them from a spontaneous cause that begets without thought or that comes to be from God and begets with discourse and divine knowledge?[75]

D THEA. Because of my age, perhaps, I often vacillate between the two. But when I look at you now and I suspect that you think that these things come to be from God, I myself think in this way.

PHIL. Very good, Theaetetus. And if we thought that you were one of those who would believe otherwise at some later date, we would try to make you agree now by the force of persuasive argument. But since I understand that your nature inclines you towards the things to which you now say you are drawn without arguments from us, I shall let that pass. For it would be a waste of time. But I shall suppose that the things we say are made by nature
E are produced by a divine art, while the things made from them by humans are produced by a human art. According to this account, there are two kinds of productive art, the human and the divine.

THEA. Correct.

PHIL. Then divide again into two each of the two.

THEA. How?

266 PHIL. Just as before, you divided the productive art horizontally, now, again, divide it vertically.

THEA. Let it be divided.

PHIL. So all the parts of it come to be four, two pertain to ourselves and are human, and two pertain to the gods and are divine.

THEA. Yes.

PHIL. When, in turn, the division has been made the other way, one part from each half could be called the part productive of a thing itself, and the remaining two could very well be called productive of an image. And in the same way the art of production is once again divided into two.

B THEA. Tell me again how each is to be divided.

PHIL. We know, I suppose, that we and the other living creatures, as well as the things of which they are by nature composed, fire and water and their kindred, all of these, are offspring of the God who has fashioned each of them. Do you agree?

THEA. I do.

PHIL. Images of each of these, but not the things themselves, accompany them, and these too have come to be by divine contrivance.

THEA. What are they?

PHIL. Semblances in dreams and those that occur during the day are said
C to be naturally produced, as is a shadow when darkness interrupts firelight, and a reflection when its own light and that of another have come together as one on bright and smooth things and fashion a form that yields a sensation contrary to the usual direct visual sensation.

THEA. So there are two works of divine production, the thing itself and the image that attends it in each case.

PHIL. What about our art? Do we not say that we produce a house itself by means of the house-building art, and another sort of house by means of the painting art, fashioned as a man-made dream for those who are awake?

D THEA. Certainly.

PHIL. Therefore, we also speak in this way of other products of our productive action as twofold: there is the thing itself and its image.

THEA. Now I understand better, and I posit two forms of production of the two sorts. There is divine and human production, according to the one division, and there is the production of the things themselves and of their likenesses according to the other.

E PHIL. Then let us recall that [we said that] if a falsehood should appear to really be a falsehood and to be of such a nature as to be some one being among others, there would be two kinds of arts of image-making, the likeness-making art and the semblance-making art.

THEA. I recall.

PHIL. So that has been shown, and for this reason shall we now, without argument, count them as two forms of the art?

THEA. Yes.

267 PHIL. Then let us again distinguish into two the semblance-making kind.

THEA. How?

PHIL. One kind of semblance comes to be by means of instruments and the other comes to be when whoever produces the semblance makes himself the instrument.

THEA. What are you saying?

PHIL. When someone uses his own body to make it appear to be similar in

appearance to yours or uses his own voice to make it sound like your voice, this part of the semblance-making art, I believe, is especially called imitation.
THEA. Yes.
PHIL. Let this art be set apart, calling it the imitative part, and indulge
B ourselves by leaving all the other parts for someone else to collect together into one by a suitable name.
THEA. Let it be sectioned off and the others be left behind.
PHIL. And again this art should be thought to be two-fold. Consider why.
THEA. You tell me.
PHIL. Some imitators know what they are imitating, others do not. Shall we suppose that there is a more important division than that between ignorance and knowledge?
THEA. Not at all.
PHIL. Was not the imitation just mentioned produced by one who knew what he was imitating? For someone who was familiar with you and your appearance would be the one to imitate you.
C THEA. Certainly.
PHIL. What of the appearance of justice or virtue taken as a whole? Do not many who are ignorant of it, but believe in it somehow, very eagerly attempt to make that in which they believe seem to be in themselves, imitating it as much as possible in their actions and discourses?
THEA. Certainly, very many do so.
PHIL. Although in no way just, not all of them fail to seem to be just, do they? Or is the contrary of this entirely the case?
THEA. The contrary.
D PHIL. Then I think that we must say that one imitator is different from another, the ignorant one from the one with knowledge.
THEA. Yes.
PHIL. Then where will someone get a suitable name for each of the two? It is clearly difficult, since, as it seems, our ancestors were for a long time idle and careless about divisions of kinds according to forms, with the result that they did not at all attempt to distinguish them, and for this reason, there cannot be a great number of names. Nonetheless, even if it is rather bold to name it, let us, for the sake of making the distinction, call imitation based
E on belief, belief-based imitation, and imitation based on knowledge, a kind of researched imitation.
THEA. Let it be so.
PHIL. Let us take up the former. For the sophist was not among those who know, but among those who imitate [those who know].

THEA. Very much so.

PHIL. Let us investigate the belief-based imitator to determine whether he is solid like iron or still has in him some sort of crack.

THEA. Let us investigate.

268 PHIL. He has a very big crack indeed. For one kind of imitator is naïve in thinking that he knows what he believes. The character of the other, because of the twists and turns of his arguments, is having a great deal of suspicion and fear that he is ignorant of what he has pretended to others to know.

THEA. Certainly there are both of these kinds of which you speak.

PHIL. Therefore, shall we suppose that one is a straightforward imitator and the other an insincere imitator?

THEA. It seems reasonable.

PHIL. Should we then say that there is one kind of insincere imitator or two?

THEA. See for yourself.

B PHIL. I shall. Two [kinds] are apparent to me. I see one who can display his insincerity in public with lengthy discourses to a large audience, and another who can display it in the private sector with short discourses and force the one to whom he speaks to say things that are contrary to themselves.

THEA. Very well said.

PHIL. Then what should we call the one who speaks at greater length, statesman or demagogue?

THEA. Demagogue.

PHIL. And what shall we call the other, sage or sophist?

THEA. I suppose that he cannot be called a sage, since we have assumed
C that he has no knowledge. But since he is an imitator of the sage, it is clear that he will receive a name derived from his. And, indeed, I now know that one must say, in truth, that that very one is in every respect really a sophist.

PHIL. Therefore, shall we bind up his name just as we have done previously, by weaving it together from the end to the beginning.

THEA. Certainly.

PHIL. It seems then, that he speaks most truly who says that the sophist in his being is one who possesses the imitator's art [of the sort] "whose descent
D and lineage"[76] is from the art of making statements [that seem to be] contrary to themselves, which is born of the insincere part of the belief-based imitation art of the semblance-making kind, which is born of the image-making art, which is a kind of human rather than divine production and whose distinctive part is verbal wonder-making.

THEA. He certainly does.

Notes

[1] See *Thea.*, 210D.

[2] Theodorus is being made to reveal to the reader that the stranger from Elea is not merely a seeker after wisdom, but one who possesses it because of his training in dialectic, which was developed by Parmenides and his students. Unlike the jury in the *Apology*, he is able to distinguish a sophist from a genuine philosopher. There are allusions to Socrates being mistaken for a sophist throughout the text.

[3] See *Odyssey*, Bk. 9, 270; Bk. 17, 483–487. Plato himself believes that the development of a just sense of shame is an important part of the philosopher's training in virtue. (*Cp. Prot.* 322C, *Phdr.* 253C–255B, *Laws* 635B-650B, esp. 646E ff. and 649A–650B.) Socrates is complimenting Theodorus and the others whom the philosopher from Elea accompanies for their development of a sense of shame. Moreover, Plato believes that the gods accompany those who practice virtue in the sense of being for those who believe in them a model of virtue to emulate. For those with a sense of shame actually to be accompanied by such a god would be a great boon, since should he observe them falter in the practice of virtue he would shame them and thereby help them to complete their training.

[4] Underlying Plato's playful suggestion that the philosopher from Elea may be a god of refutation is that he may be a sophist, who is able to pretend to possess the knowledge of a god because he can refute what we say by exploiting our carelessness in the use of discourse. It is this appearance of possessing divine wisdom because of skill in exploiting our carelessness in discourse that Plato wishes to dispel in the *Sophist*.

[5] The godlike philosopher is he who has, by the practice of dialectic, ascended to knowledge of the nature of the Good. (*Cp. Rep.* 511B–C) We practice the philosophy of Plato so that we may become godlike. (*Cp. Phd.* 80D–81A, 82B–C, 84A–B)

[6] The kind to which a godlike philosopher belongs is just about as difficult to define as the kind to which a god belongs. The failure to discern the nature of a god in fact has occasioned the sorts of stories of misconduct Homer and other poets tell of the gods, and the acceptance of such stories inhibits our practice of the virtues because we by nature tend to emulate the gods.

[7] *Cp. Odyssey,* Bk. 17, 486.

[8] Plato, and his student, Aristotle, protest the poets' representations of the gods as envious of mortals who should possess their wisdom. Since the philosopher has been playfully called a god here, Plato has Theodorus add that since he is godlike, and so, like the gods, is without envy, he is willing to share his wisdom. Pindar and the Greek tragedians ascribed to the gods envy at the great prosperity of men.

[9] The Stranger goes along with the playful allusion to himself as a god without envy.

[10] Plato often brings up the question of the appropriateness and length of the kind of discourse used for a specific purpose. (*Cp. Phdr., Pol., Rep.*, and *Phd.*)

[11] The point is that the respondent be willing and able to understand a philosopher's questions and give honest answers, not that he will say whatever the philosopher wants him to say.

[12] Why does it seem best to the philosopher to begin by seeking the definition of the nature of a

sophist? He was playfully likened to a sophist by Socrates at the beginning of the discussion because the philosopher often appears to others to be a sophist. Perhaps he thinks that a philosopher's nature is more difficult to discern than that of a sophist because a philosopher is more easily mistaken for a sophist and it is therefore more difficult to get agreement from a student about what a philosopher is than it is to get his agreement about what a sophist is. Or perhaps he thinks that defining the nature of a sophist is a way to better facilitate the dialectical process of leading the student to a definition of the nature of a philosopher.

[13] This is a key point. It is our failure to disambiguate names that most often enables the sophist to formulate refutations of our claims in which these names occur.

[14] This does not mean that they will practice on something that is unimportant, but on something whose likeness to something else does not lead to a confusion with it, as the likeness of a sophist to a philosopher leads to a confusion of a philosopher with a sophist.

[15] An angler is not worth the serious attention of the philosopher because he is not confused with something else that he is like.

[16] The method by which the undeceptive nature of the angler is to be revealed will be used to reveal the deceptive nature of the sophist.

[17] In the *Phaedrus* at 270D Socrates says that to show the nature of anything we must determine whether it is simple or comprised of parts, and if simple, determine what are its powers of acting on something else or being acted on by something else and by what means these powers are exercised; and if complex, we should determine what its parts are, and analyze them in the same way. The case of an angler is used because the form of an angler is easier to distinguish, since both the powers of an angler to act on something else and the means by which these powers are exercised are well-known. Plato, like Aristotle, divides powers into those that are rational and those that are irrational, and among the rational powers, there are skills or arts (*technai*), which pertain to the use of reason to perform actions well, and forms of knowledge (*epistēmai*), which pertain to the use of reason to think correctly. Plato has the philosopher begin from the primary genus of angling, which is an exercise of skill or art.

[18] The objects acquired by the arts of learning or acquiring knowledge are goods for the rational part of the soul, the objects acquired by the art of acquiring money are goods for the appetitive part of the soul, and the objects acquired by the arts of competing against other for things and hunting things are goods for the spirited part of the soul. Among those that acquire their objects by conquest, the art of competing against others for things also requires the art of preventing oneself from being conquered by others.

[19] So the first division proceeds by distinguishing two ways in which the skill can be exercised, by acquiring things or by producing them.

[20] The philosopher divides the genus by reference to two means by which the power to acquire things is exercised, in accord with the account of how to arrive at a definition in the *Phaedrus* passage cited above.

[21] The art of hunting is divided by the two basic kinds of things that can be hunted, lifeless things and living things. Plants are not included among the living things, presumably, because they are not

in hiding, and hence, are not hunted, but gathered.

[22] This division of living hunted things is based on their bodily parts and their suitability to their environment. Snakes are included among the water animals because they are without feet, and are designed by nature to swim rather than to travel on land. And that some snakes actually live on land, for Plato, is contrary to nature, and probably brought about because of some abnormal condition. Birds are not by nature air or sky animals, even though most of them can fly, since they do not live in the sky, but either on the land, in which case they have feet, or on the water, in which case they have something analogous to fins where other birds have feet.

[23] This division is made by reference to the two basic kinds of water animals hunted, those with wings and those with fins, the former living on the water and the latter in the water.

[24] In this case the division is made by reference to the kind of instrument used to exercise the skill being divided.

[25] Again, the division is made by reference to the different means by which the skill is exercised. In fire lighting the fire itself is used to lure the fish to the fisherman's hooked spear, while in hooking something else is used to attract the fish.

[26] The final division will be made by reference to how the fish is acted upon by the instrument used to acquire it.

[27] The *idiōtēs*, in its root meaning, is a self-sufficient private citizen, or non-professional who takes no part in the affairs of the city-state. Here it is equivalent to being unskilled, and refers to someone who does not take part in any art of production or acquisition.

[28] Perhaps this is an allusion to the view that a sophist's art may in fact be a knack (*Cp. Gorg.*, 461B–466A).

[29] The philosopher begins the process of getting the student of dialectic to distinguish the many different parts of a sophist's kind as the first step in the attempt to show his nature.

[30] When the student questions the philosopher's suggestion about how to divide a genus, the philosopher is to interrupt the process of division for the purpose of arguing for the subdivision he has suggested. In this case, the philosopher need only point out the alternatives, none of which is plausible.

[33] Theaetetus shows his quickness by seeing, from a mere enumeration of the alternatives, that a subdivision suggested by the philosopher is valid. The philosopher does not pause to make an explicit division of tame animals into those that both sense and think objects and those that only sense objects. He proceeds immediately to one half of the division previously made because in his last comment to Theaetetus he already introduced human beings as the subdivision of tame animals.

[32] This is a collection of the different species of persuasion by words.

[33] This is not a division by the place where persuasion by words is used, but by the type of persuasive discourse appropriate to such places. The kind appropriate in a private gathering is not appropriate in a public gathering. The arts of forensic speech and public speaking belong to second

kind, the art of private conversation to the first.

[34] The philosopher's elucidation of this division in 222E indicates that it is ultimately made by reference to the manner in which the hunter hunts, which is either by luring his prey with gifts or by flattering them for the sake of being supported by them.

[35] The lover's art has many forms, one of which is the art of hunting for a beloved in private gatherings by persuading him with words and gifts. The lover's art, however, is not a subdivision of the art of hunting.

[36] This division of the genus is made by reference to the type of payment and the effect produced by the discourse used to persuade.

[37] The philosopher is probably made to omit the subdivision of the art of hunting the young into the art of hunting them by means of persuasive speech because that aspect of his art, if emphasized here, would naturally lead to questions of how he does this. This question will be raised later, after other aspects of his art are explored.

[38] He means that they were led, in following out one branch of a division, to end up mentioning a skill belonging to another.

[39] The way in which he will follow the trail is by dividing the different kinds of differentiae used to divide the primary genera to which the sophist's skills belong. These differentiae are comprised of pairs of contraries of different sorts, among which are separating things and combining them. In the *Statesman* separating things and combining them are said to be of universal application.

[40] The translation of this sentence is painfully literal, and does not represent how it would, in other contexts, be translated, which is as "He who speaks of non-something is speaking of nothing at all." The literal translation of *mēden* as "non-one" is made necessary by the previous statement in the argument that what is something is what is one, so that here, by placing "non" before "something," the placing of "non" before "one" is justified. Readers should realize that *mēden* in Greek is used as "nothing" is used in English. I italicize "non" before "one" in order to capture the use of *pantapasi* to emphasize the negative force of "non" in "non-one."

[41] See the commentary for a reconstruction of the argument.

[42] The first principle upon which Parmenides' statement of the difficulty about non-being is based seems to be that non-being itself cannot be a being.

[43] Theaetetus' statement is ambiguous. He means to be saying that an image is not at all a real thing of which it is the likeness, not that it is not at all a real thing. His failure to add the qualification, "of which it is the likeness," will enable the philosopher, who is taking the role of a sophist to change its meaning. Ordinarily, in an argument it is the sophist who drops a qualification his interlocutor adds to what is asserted or denied of a subject so that he can change the meaning of what is asserted or denied of the subject in order to draw a problematic conclusion. In this case, Plato has Theaetetus loosely answer the question he was asked in order to change the meaning of what Theaetetus meant to say.

[44] Something really is a being (*ontōs on*) if it partakes of being.

[45] The philosopher here substitutes "likeness" for "image" because of the common practice of using the name of the most important species of a genus for the name of the genus itself.

[46] Here I translate *ouk on* from W. In B *oukon* appears. The implication is that the definition of the nature of an image has implied that it partakes of non-being. Theaetetus, therefore, immediately protests that it is in some way a being. The reason is then given that it must be a being because it is a likeness, which is a being.

[47] Here I take *doxadsousa* to mean "believing to be" rather than simply "believing," just as I have translated *phainesthai* and *dokein* at 236E1 as "appearing to be" and "seeming to be" rather than "appearing" and "seeming," respectively. Some translators translate this sentence, as well as similar sentences to follow, in a way that hides the use of the negative sign to negate *onta* (the plural of *on*).

[48] To believe that non-beings are beings is to believe that non-beings *in relation to the subject of the belief* are beings *in relation to the subject of the belief.* Flying, e.g. is a non-being in relation to Theaetetus, who is being believed to fly.

[49] The use of *medamōs* here and below instead of *mē* is indicated in the translation by italicizing "non-" in "non-X." There is no way in English to accentuate the use of the negative sign when used to negate a term.

[50] At 243B.

[51] The Greek of this sentence has no fixed sense. Most scholars seem to believe that it is corrupted. I follow Cornford here in assuming that the sentence is better left untranslated than given a highly speculative interpretation.

[52] Cadmus was said to have sown the teeth of a dragon he killed and from the sown teeth his warriors were said to have been born.

[53] That is, the mind would once again not be a being.

[54] The difficulty is that now being too has proved to be unnamable and unthinkable. However, when the philosopher infers that being is neither in motion nor at rest, from the premise that being, according to its own nature, is neither in motion nor at rest, he is assuming that the only way in which being could be in motion or at rest is according to its own nature. He is about to argue that this is not so. According to its own nature, he believes, being is only a being. Being is in motion and at rest, he will imply, later in the dialogue, only by virtue of partaking of motion and rest.

[55] Eurycles was a famous ventriloquist.

[56] Motion, as a form, is the ultimate subject of motion, the nature, and it cannot be at rest. Similarly, rest, as a form, is the ultimate subject of rest, the nature, and it cannot be in motion.

[57] The nature of the other is otherness, which it possesses only in relation to something else. Plato can refer to the other as the nature of the other because the form and its nature are not other than one another.

[58] The nature of the other has not been proved to pervade all of the five kinds, but only to pervade

being, motion and rest. See the introduction for the explanation.

[59] From the admission that motion is completely other than rest, which is at rest, the philosopher concludes that motion is a non-rest in the sense that it partakes of the other than a thing that is at rest.

[60] Theaetetus is made to use *oudamōs* to accentuate the negative sign that occurred before "rest," because motion is contrary to rest.

[61] At 255E.

[62] Since motion has just been shown to be a non-being that is a being, it is concluded that, in relation to motion, a non-being is a being.

[63] In other words, all forms other than being are beings that are non-beings. In a moment the philosopher will add that being itself partakes of non-being.

[64] The nature of the other renders each of the forms other than being a non-being in the sense that each is made to be that which is other than a being to which it is contrasted, which in this case is the form, being, which is a being by its own nature. Hence, I translate *mē on* as "a non-being" rather than as "non-being," even though it has been concluded that non-being must be a being in relation both to motion and to all the kinds other than being. To say that non-being must be a being in relation to these forms means that non-being must be predicated of them, since they are non-beings.

[65] In other words, each form, other than being itself, is many beings insofar as it partakes of many beings, and is countless non-beings insofar as it is other than all of the beings other than being itself. See the introduction for a more detailed explanation.

[66] Plato does not imply, as some assume he does, that what is non-large must be either small or equal in size, only that a negated term does not signify what is contrary to that which is signified by the term itself.

[67] The nature of the other, just as the nature of knowledge, is what it is in relation to something else. The nature of the other is divided into parts, each of which is being other in relation to a different thing. The nature of knowledge is divided into parts, each of which is knowledge in relation to a different thing.

[68] Just as the different parts of knowledge are distinguished by the different kinds of objects of knowledge, so the different parts of the nature of the other are distinguished by the different kinds of forms in relation to which a thing is other than something else.

[69] A contrast (*antithesis*) to the beautiful is an otherness than something else in relation to its beauty.

[70] The obscurity of this statement seem to be due to Plato's attempt to make reference to what is beautiful regardless whether it is beautiful by its own nature or by partaking of the beautiful. To be other than nothing other than the nature of the beautiful does not mean to not be beautiful or to not be the beautiful, but to other than something that is a beautiful thing.

[71] The part of the nature of the other that is set in contrast to a part of the nature of being is the nature, being other than something that is a being, just as the part of the nature of the other that is set is

contrast to the nature of the beautiful is that which is other than something that is beautiful.

[72] The contrast to being with respect to each thing is the contrast to the being of each thing, i.e. to every other being.

[73] The terms *doxa* and *logos* can mean either believing and saying or what is believed and what is said, and in the present argument they can only mean what is believed and what is said.

[74] In this and the following sentences I translate *legei* as "reports" rather than as "says," since it is better English and is one of its meanings. This translation could also have been used at 262D5, where *legein* is used to distinguish *logos* ("discourse") from *onoma* ("name").

[75] The contrast, as is clear from *Laws* X, is between a cause such as the four elements, which beget without thought, and a cause such as the soul, which begets with discourse and divine knowledge because of its own divine origin.

[76] See Homer, *Iliad*, Zeta, line 211.

Bibliography

Except for the Greek text, this bibliography lists only works in English. There many more books and articles in other Western languages.

The Greek Text

Platonis Opera - Recognovit brevique adnotatione critica instruxerunt E. A Duke, W. F. Hicken, W. S. M. Nicoll, D. B. Robinson, J. C. G. Strachan, vol. I (which included *Euthyphro, Apologia, Crito, Phaedo, Cratylus, Theaetetus, Sophista,* and *Politicus*), Oxford: Oxford University Press 1995 (a revision of the edition was published by John Burnet, 1900–7).

Translations of the Sophist

Brann, Eva. T. *Plato's Sophist: the Professor of Wisdom.* Focus Publishing, R. Pullins Company, 1966

Cobb, William S. *Plato's Sophist.* United States: Rowman & Littlefield Publishers, Inc. 1990.

Cornford, F. M. *Plato's Theory of Knowledge, the Theaetetus and Sophist of Plato.* London: Routledge and Kegan Paul, 1935.

Fowler, Harold North. *Plato: Theaetetus and Sophist.* Cambridge, Mass.: Harvard University Press, 1961

Jowett, Benjamin, Plato's *Sophist*, in *The Dialogues of Plato*, 4th ed., revised by D. J. Allan and H. E. Dale. Oxford: Oxford University Press, 1953.

Matthews, Gwynneth. *Plato's Epistemology and Related Logical Problems.* New York: Humanities Press, 1972 (contains a translation of 232B–264B of the *Sophist*).

Taylor, A. E. *Plato: The Sophist and the Statesman.* New York: Thomas Nelson and Sons, 1961.

Warrington, J. *Plato, Parmenides Theaetetus, the Sophist, the Statesman.* London, 1961.

White, Nicholaus. *Plato's Sophist*. Indianapolis: Hackett, 1993

Commentaries and Extensive Studies of the Sophist

Ambuel, David. *Image and paradigm in Plato's Sophist.* La Vegas: Parmenides Publishing Company 2007

Benardete, Seth. *The Being of the Beautiful: Plato's Theaetetus, Sophist and Statesman.* Chicago: University of Chicago Press, 1984.

Bluck, Richard S. *Plato's Sophist,* edited with extensive introduction by Gordon C. Neal. Manchester, 1975

Campbell, Rev. Lewis. *Sophistes and Politicus of Plato, with a revised text and English notes.* Oxford: the Clarendon Press, 1867. Reprint New York: Arno Press, 1973.

Cornford, F. M. *Plato's Theory of Knowledge. The Theaetetus and Sophist of Plato.* London: Routledge and Kegan Paul, 1935.

Crombie, I. M. *An Examination of Plato's Doctrines, II Plato on Knowledge and Reality.* London: Routledge & Kegan Paul, 1963, pp. 388–422.

Gale, R. *Negation and Not-Being*, in *American Philosophical Quarterly Monograph Series* 10. Oxford: Blackwell, 1975.
Heidegger, M. *Plato's Sophist,* translated by Richard Rojcewicz and Andre Schuwer. Bloomington and Indianapolis: Indiana University Press, 1997.
Kamlah, W. *Platons Selbstkritik im Sophistes*. Zetemata, Heft 33,München, 1963.
Ketchum, Richard. *Truth and Being in Plato's Sophist.* Philadelphia: University of Pennsylvania Press 1971.
Klein, J. *Plato's Trilogy, Theaetetus, the Sophist and the Statesman*. Chicago, 1977.
McCabe, M. M. *Plato's Individuals*. Princeton: Princeton University Press, 1994, 192–243.
Notomi, N. *The Unity of Plato's Sophist*. Cambridge: Cambridge University Press, 2001.
Patterson, R. *Image and Reality in Plato's Metaphysics*. Indianapolis: Hackett Publishing Company, 1985.
Pelletier, F. J. *Parmenides, Plato, and the Semantics of Not-Being*. Chicago: University of Chicago Press, 1990.
Ray, A. Chadwick. *For Images, an Interpretation of Plato's Sophist*. University Press of America, 1984,
Rijk, L. M. *Plato's Sophist. A Philosophical Commentary*. Amsterdam: North-Holland Publishing Company, 1986.
Rosen, Stanley. *Plato's Sophist. The Drama of Original and Image*. New Haven: Yale University Press, 1983.
Runciman, W. *Plato's Later Epistemology*. Cambridge: Cambridge University Press, 1965.
Sayre, K. *Plato's Analytic Method*. Chicago: University of Chicago Press, 1969, 138–215.
———. *Plato's Late Ontology: a Riddle Resolved*. Princeton: Princeton University Press, 1983. Second edition: Parmenides Publishing, 2005 with a new introduction and essay.
Seligman, P. *Being and Not-Being: an Introduction to Plato's Sophist*. The Hague: Nijhoff, 1974.
Swindler, James Kenneth. *Plato's Sophist and Contemporary Analytic Ontology.* Lawrence: University of Kansas Press, 1978.

Articles and Discussions in Books

Ackrill, J. L. "*Symplokē eidōn*." *Bulletin of the Institute of Classical Studies of the University of London* 2, 1955, 31–5. Reprinted in Allen, R.E., ed. *Studies in Plato's Metaphysics* London: Routledge & Kegan Paul, 1965, pp. 199–206, and in Vlastos, Gregory, ed. *Plato I: Metaphysics and Epistemology.* Garden City: Anchor Books, 1970, 201–9.
———."Plato and the Copula." *Journal of Hellenic Studies*, 77: 1–6, 1957. Reprinted in Allen, R.E. *Studies in Plato's Metaphysics*, London, Routledge & Kegan Paul, 1965, pp. 207–18, Vlastos, Gregory, ed. *Plato I: Metaphysics and Epistemology.* Garden City: Anchor Books, 1970, 210–22 and in Ackrill, John. *Essays on Plato and Aristotle.* Oxford, Clarendon Press, 1997.
Benardete, Seth. "Plato *Sophist* 223b1–7." *Phronesis* 5, 1960, 129–39.
———. "On Plato's *Sophist.*" *Review of Metaphysics* 46, 1993, 747–80. Reprinted in Seth Benardete, *The Argument of the Action: Essays on Greek Poetry and Philosophy.* Chicago, University of Chicago Press, 2000.
Berger, F. R. "Rest and Motion in the Sophist." *Phronesis* 10, 1965, 70–7.

Bolton, Robert, "Plato's distinction between Being and Becoming." *Review of Metaphysics* 29, 1975, 66–95. Reprinted in N. D. Smith, ed. *Plato. Critical Assessments Vol. II: Plato's Middle Period: Metaphysics and Epistemology.* London: Routledge, 1998, 116-41.

Bodeson, William, "Some problems about being and predication in Plato's *Sophist* 242–49." *Journal of the History of Philosophy* 14, 1976, 1–10.

Bostock, D. "Plato on 'is not.'" *Oxford Studies in Ancient Philosophy* 2, 1984, 89–119.

Brown, L. "*Being in the Sophist: A Syntactical Enquiry.*" *Oxford Studies in Ancient Philosophy* 4, 1986, 49–70.

Crombie, I. M. *An Examination of Plato's Doctrines, II: Plato on Knowledge and Reality.* London, 1963, 401–10.

Dancy Russell M., "The Categories of Being in Plato's *Sophist* 255c-e." *Ancient Philosophy* 19, 1999, 45–72.

Denyer, N. *Language, Thought and Falsehood in Ancient Greek Philosophy.* London and New York: Routledge, 1991, 128–145.

De Vries, William, "On *Sophist* 255b-e." *History of Philosophy Quarterly* 5, 1988, 385–94.

Ferg, S. "Plato on False Statement: Relative Being, A Part of Being, and Not-Being in the *Sophist*." *Journal of the History of Philosophy* 14, 1960, 336–42.

Flower, R. J. "G. E. L. Owen, Plato, and the Verb 'To Be.'" *Apeiron*, 14. 87–95.

Frede, M. "Plato's *Sophist* on false statements," in R. Kraut, ed. *The Cambridge Companion to Plato.* Cambridge: Cambridge University Press, 1992.

———. "The literary form of the *Sophist*," In *Form and Argument in Late Plato.* Ed. by Gill, Christopher and McCabe, Mary Margaret. Oxford: Oxford University Press, 1996, 135–52

Furth, M. "Elements of Eleatic Ontology." *Journal of the History of Philosophy* 6, 1968, 111–32. Reprinted in A. Mourelatos, *The Presocratics.* New York: Anchor Books, 1974, 241–70.

Gerson, Lloyd. "A distinction in Plato's *Sophist*." *Classical Quarterly* 63, 1986, 251–66. Reprinted in Smith, Nicholas D., ed. *Plato. Critical Assessments: Plato's Later Works,* vol. IV. London: Routledge, 1998, 125–41.

Gomez-Lobo, Alfonso. "Plato Description of Dialectic in the *Sophist* 253d1–e2." *Phronesis* 22, 1977, 29–47.

Gulley, N. *Plato's Theory of Knowledge.* London, 1962.

Hackforth, R. "False Statement in the *Sophist*." *Classical Quarterly* 39, 56–8, 1945.

Hamlyn, D. "The Communion of Forms and the Development of Plato's Logic." *Philosophical Quarterly* 5, 1955, 289–302.

Heinaman, R. "Being in the *Sophist*." *Archiv für Geshichte der Philosophie* 65, 1983, 1–17.

———. "Self-Predication in the *Sophist*." Phronesis, 1981, 55–66.

———. "Once more: Being in the *Sophist*." *Archiv für Geschichte der Philosophie* 68, 1986, 121–5.

Hestir, B. E. "A 'Conception' of Truth in Plato's *Sophist*." *Journal of the History of Philosophy* 41, 2003, 1–24.

Jordan, Robert William, "Plato's task in the *Sophist*." *Classical Quarterly* 34, 1984, 113–29.

Kahn, C. H. "Some Philosophical Uses of 'to be' in Plato." *Phronesis* 26, 1981 105–34.

———. "Being in Parmenides and Plato." *Parola del Passato* 43, 1988, 237–61.

Kerferd, G. B. "Plato's Noble Art of Sophistry." *Classical Quarterly* 4, 1954, 84–90.

Ketchum, R. "Participation and Predication in *Sophist* 251–60." *Phronesis* 23, 1978, 42–63.

Keyt, D. "Plato's Paradox that the Immutable is Unknowable." *The Philosophical Quarterly* 19, 1969, 1–14.

———. "The Falsity of 'Theaetetus Flies' (*Sophist* 263B)." In *Exegesis and Argument*, ed. Lee, E., Mourelatos, A. and Rorty, R. *Phronesis* Supplementary Volume 1, 1973, 285–305.

Kirwin, C. "Falsehood Unmasked." *Phronesis* 36, 1991, 319–27.

Kostman, J. "False Logos and Not-Being in Plato's *Sophist*." In Moravcsik, J. M. E. *Patterns in Plato's Thought*. Dordrecht: Reidel, 1973, 193–212.

———. "The ambiguity of 'partaking' in Plato's *Sophist*." *Journal of the History of Philosophy* 27, 1989, 343–63.

Lacey, Alan Robert, "Plato's *Sophist* and the Forms." *Classical Quarterly* 9, 1959, 43–52.

Lee, E. N. "Plato on Negation and Not-being in the *Sophist*." *Philosophical Review* 81, 1972, 267–304.

Lewis, F. "Did Plato Discover the *estin* of Identity?" *California Studies in Classical Antiquity* 8 (1975), 113–43.

———. "Plato on 'Not'." *California Studies in Classical Antiquity* 9, 1976, 89–115.

McDowell, J. "Falsehood and Not-Being in Plato's *Sophist*." in M. Schofield and M. Nussbaum, *Language and Logos*. Cambridge: Cambridge University Press, 1982, 115–34.

Malcolm, J. "Plato's Analysis of *to on* and *to mē on* in the *Sophist*." *Phronesis* 12, 1967, 130–46.

———. "Being in the *Sophist*." *Archiv für Geschichte der Philosophie* 1983, 1–17.

———. "Does Plato Revise his Ontology in *Sophist* 246c–249d?" *Archiv für Geschichte der Philosophie,* 1983, 115–27.

———. "Remarks on an Incomplete Rendering of Being in the *Sophist*." *Archiv für Geschichte der Philosophie*, 1985, 162–65.

———. "On 'what is not in any way' in the *Sophist*." *Classical Quarterly* 35, 1985, 520–23.

Mates, B. "Identity and Predication in Plato." *Phronesis,* 1979, 211–29.

Matthen, M. "Greek Ontology and the 'Is' of Truth." *Phronesis* 28, 1983, 113–35.

McDowell, John. "Falsehood and Not-being in Plato's *Sophist,"* in *Language and Logos. Studies in ancient Greek philosophy presented to G. E. L. Owen.* Edited by Schofield, Malcolm and Nussbaum, Martha. Cambridge: Cambridge University Press, 1982. 115–34.

Moravcsik, J. "*Symplokē eidōn* and the Genesis of *logos*," *Archiv für Geshichte der Philosophie* 42 (1960), 117–29.

———. "Being and Meaning in the *Sophist*," *Acta Philosophica Fennica*, Fasc. XIV, 1962, 23–78.

———. "Critical Notice of P. Seligman, *Being and Not-Being*." *Canadian Journal of Philosophy* 4, 1976, 37–44.

Mourelatos, Alexander. "'Nothing' as 'Not-Being': Some Literary Contexts that Bear on Plato," in *Arktouros. Hellenic Studies Presented to Bernard M. W. Knox on the Occasion of his 65th Birthday.* ed. by Bowersock, Glen, Burkert, Walter and Putnam, Michael. Berlin: Walter de Gruyter, 1979. 319–29. Reprinted in Anton, J. P., Preus, A., eds. *Essays in Ancient Greek Philosophy*, vol. 2. Albany: State University of New York Press, 1983, 59–69.

O'Rourke, F. "Plato's Approach to Being in the *Theaetetus* and *Sophist*, and Heidegger's Attribution of Aristotelian influence." *Diotima*, 31 (2003), 47–58.

Owen, G. E. L. "Plato on Not-Being." in Vlastos, Gregory., ed. *Plato I: Metaphysics and Epistemology* Garden City: Anchor Books, 1968, 223–67.

Peck, A "Plato and the *megista genē* of the *Sophist*." *Classical Quarterly* 2, 1952, 32–56.

———. "Plato's *Sophist*: the *symplokē tōn eidōn*." *Phronesis* 7, 1962, 46–66.

———. "Plato versus Parmenides." *Philosophical Review* 71, 1962, 159–84.

Philip, J. "False Statement in the *Sophistes*." *Transactions and Proceedings of the American Philosophical Society* 70, 1968, 315–27.

Pippin, R. "Negation and Not Being in Wittgenstein's *Tractatus* and Plato's *Sophist*." *Kantstudien* 70, 1979, 179–96.

Prior, W. J. "Plato's Analysis of Being and Not-Being in the *Sophist*." *Southern Journal of Philosophy* 18, 1980, 199–211.

Roberts, Jean. "The problem about Being in the *Sophist*." *History of Philosophy Quarterly* 3, 1986, 229–43. Reprinted in Smith, Nicholas D., ed. *Plato, Critical Assessments, Plato's Later Works* vol. IV, London: Routledge, 1998, 142–57.

Robinson, D. B. "Textual Notes on Plato's *Sophist*." *The Classical Quarterly*, 49, 1999.

Ross, D. Plato's *Theory of Ideas*. Oxford: Oxford University Press, 1951.

Sayre, K. "Falsehood, Forms and Participation in the *Sophist*." *Noûs* 4, 1970, 81–91.

———. "*Sophist* 263B Revisited." *Mind* 85, 1976, 581–86.

Schipper, E. "The Meaning of Existence in Plato's *Sophist*." *Phronesis* 9, 1964, 38–44.

Simon, Derek. "The *Sophist*, 246a–259e: *Ousia* and *to on* in Plato's Ontologies." *De Philosophia* 12, 1996, 155–77.

Swindler, James Kenneth, "Parmenides' Paradox." *Review of Metaphysics* 33, 1980, 727–44.

Teloh, H. *The Development of Plato's Metaphysics*. University Park: Pennsylvania State University Press, 1981, 189–204.

Thom, Paul. "Critical notice of F. J. Pelletier's *Parmenides, Plato, and the Semantics of Not-Being*." *Canadian Journal of Philosophy* 22, 1992, 573–86.

Thorp, John. "Forms, Concepts and *to mē on*," *Revue de Philosophie Ancienne* 2. 1984, 77–92.

Trevaskis, J. R. "*The megista genē and the Vowel Analogy of Plato*." Acta Univ. Stockholmiensis 17, Stockholm, 1977.

Turnbull, R. "The Argument of the *Sophist*." *Philosophical Quarterly* 14, 1964, 23–34.

Van Eck, J. "Falsity without Negative Predication: On *Sophistes* 255e–263d." *Phronesis* 40, 1995, 20–47.

van Fraassen, B. "Logical Structure in Plato's *Sophist*." *Review of Metaphysics* 22, 1969, 482–98.

Vlastos, G. "An Ambiguity in the *Sophist*." In *Platonic Studies*, ed. G. Vlastos. Princeton: Princeton University Press, 1973, 270–322.

Wiggins, D. "Sentence Meaning, Negation, and Plato's Problem of Not-Being," in Vlastos, Gregory, ed. *Plato I: Metaphysics and Epistemology*. Garden City: Anchor Books, 1968, 268–303.

Xenakis, J. "Plato's *Sophist*: A Defense of Negative Expressions and a Doctrine of Sense and of Truth." *Phronesis* 4, 1959, 29–43.